THE FAMILY AT GILJE
A DOMESTIC STORY OF THE FORTIES

BY
JONAS LIE

TRANSLATED FROM THE NORWEGIAN
BY SAMUEL COFFIN EASTMAN
WITH AN INTRODUCTION BY JULIUS EMIL OLSON

NEW YORK
THE AMERICAN-SCANDINAVIAN FOUNDATION
LONDON: HUMPHREY MILFORD
OXFORD UNIVERSITY PRESS
1920

Copyright, 1920, by The American-Scandinavian Foundation

D. B. Updike · The Merrymount Press · Boston · U.S.A.

In the interest of creating a more extensive selection of rare historical book reprints, we have chosen to reproduce this title even though it may possibly have occasional imperfections such as missing and blurred pages, missing text, poor pictures, markings, dark backgrounds and other reproduction issues beyond our control. Because this work is culturally important, we have made it available as a part of our commitment to protecting, preserving and promoting the world's literature. Thank you for your understanding.

Preface

To the Honorable Samuel Coffin Eastman, of Concord, New Hampshire, belongs the credit of having given American readers an English version of *The Family at Gilje* while the author was still at the height of his creative activity. Mr. Eastman, who was a lawyer by profession, was a man of varied interests, the author of a White Mountain Guide which has gone through numerous editions, and the translator of Brandes's *Impressions of Russia* and *Poland*. He was familiar with the translations by Mrs. Ole Bull of Jonas Lie's *The Pilot and His Wife* and *The Good Ship Future*. *The Family at Gilje* was called to his attention by Miss Amalia Krohg, of Christiania, and it charmed him so much that he rendered it into English. The translation appeared serially in the Concord magazine, *The Granite Monthly*, in 1894, and was illustrated with views from Valders, the mountain district where the scene of the story is laid.

When the Committee on Publications decided to include *The Family at Gilje* in the SCANDINAVIAN CLASSICS, their attention was called to Mr. Eastman's excellent version, and permission was secured to reprint it. The translator consented to a revision of his text so as to make it conform to the general style of the CLASSICS and to interpret more accurately some of the Norwegian idioms. His death, in 1917, prevented his coöperation in the work of revision, to which, nevertheless, he had given his cordial assent.

HANNA ASTRUP LARSEN

Introduction

THE story of Jonas Lie's life, even though told in brief, will readily yield the key to the various phases of his strange authorship. No one of his long list of books is an adequate index of his powers. The special character of each is the outgrowth of peculiar traits of natural endowment in conjunction with definite facts and experiences of his life. Some of the features of his genius seem strangely incongruous — as different as day and night. These features are clearly reflected in his writings. By critics he has been variously proclaimed "the poet of Nordland," "the novelist of the sea," or "the novelist of Norwegian homes," and is commonly classed as a realist. His reputation and great popularity rest mainly upon his realistic novels. In this field he ranks as one of the leading portrayers of character and social conditions in modern Norse literature; and of his realism *The Family at Gilje* is possibly the best illustration.

Yet there was much more than an ingenuous realist in Lie.[1] He was also a fascinating mystic; a teller of fantastic stories, profoundly symbolic in character; a great myth-making *raconteur* of grotesque tales that have a distinct folkloristic flavor,

[1] Pronounced as Lee in English.

particularly as found in his two volumes entitled *Trold*. This part of his authorship, though it does not bulk large, and, naturally enough, has not been fathomed by the general reader, is nevertheless a very important part, and is surely the most original and poetic. It appears in a definite though restrained form as mystic romanticism in his first prose work, *Second Sight*, and then scarcely a trace of it is seen until it bursts forth, twenty years later, with the vigor of long-repressed passion.

It would therefore be unfair to judge Jonas Lie by the single novel in hand—as unfair as it would be to judge Ibsen by a single one of his social dramas—*The Pillars of Society*, for instance. In Ibsen the imaginative power displayed in *Brand* and *Peer Gynt* did not in the social dramas reassert itself in anything but an adumbration of the abandon and exuberance of the dramatic poems. In Lie, however, the mystic and myth-maker reappeared with strength redoubled. Erik Lie, in a book on his father's life (*Oplevelser*), says with reference to this: "If it had been given to Jonas Lie to continue his authorship in his last years, his Nordland nature would surely—such is my belief—more and more have asserted itself, and he would have dived down into the misty world of the subconscious, where his near-sighted eyes saw so clearly, and whence his first works sprang up like fantastic plants on the bottom of the sea." There is not a trace or an inkling of this clairvoyant power in *The Family at Gilje*. Its excellences are of a distinctly different nature.

This much, then, must be said to warn the reader against a too hasty appraisement of Lie's genius — his power, range, and vision — on the basis of a single novel. Let him be assured that Jonas Lie stands worthily by the side of Ibsen and Björnson both as a creative author and as a personality. He was of their generation, knew them both well as young men and old, and was a loyal friend to both, as they were to him. He even knew Björnson well enough in the early sixties to give him pointed advice on his authorship. Though he seems never to have taken such liberties with Ibsen, — as Björnson so categorically did during the same decade, — he did lend him a helping hand by paying him in advance for the dramatic poem, *Love's Comedy*, published in a periodical owned by Lie. It is interesting to note that Ibsen, so punctilious in later years, was aggravatingly slow in forwarding the final batch of manuscript. As a last resource, Lie threatened to complete the drama himself. Later in life, during summer sojourns in the Bavarian Alps, they saw much of each other. In one of his social dramas, *An Enemy of the People*, Ibsen used Lie, together with traits of

Björnson and Apothecary Thaulow (father of the painter) as a model for the genial hero, Dr. Stockmann. Both Ibsen and Björnson were generous in their praise of Lie's many fine qualities. In the sixties, before Lie had written a single novel, Björnson, in an address at Tromsö, in Arctic Norway, where Lie had spent several years of his boyhood, said some striking things about Lie's creative powers. On a later occasion he referred to him as "the great vague possibility," and after Lie's death, in a letter to the family, he said: "I have so much to thank him for. In the luxuriant wealth of my youth he was the purest in heart, the richest in fancy." Björnson understood from the first the clairvoyant mysticism in Lie, and profited by it. In other words, a man who could interest men like Ibsen and Björnson and maintain their admiration and respect for half a century could do so only by dint of rare personal powers.

Although he did not begin his literary career until he was getting on toward forty, at which age both Ibsen and Björnson had won fame, Lie, it may fairly be said, eventually overtook them in the favor of the Scandinavian reading public, and it is not unlikely that with this public he will hold his own in comparison with them. This is surely due to the realism of his social novels. Though he at times roamed far afield from the standards of realism, as has been indicated, he never was identified with extremists in any literary school, despite the sweeping force of popular currents. As a realist he was a patient plodder, following his own instincts, and in the course of long years he hammered out a literary vehicle distinctly his own, so surcharged, in fact, with the idiosyncrasies of his individuality as to make it most difficult to recast in a foreign idiom.

From the above it will appear that Lie was an interesting dual personality. Further consideration of his life will show that he was both romanticist, or mystic, and realist by right of blood, as well as through environment and personal experience.

Scandinavian romanticism began in Denmark with the opening of the nineteenth century, as a revival of the past, the exploitation of Northern antiquities for modern literary material. In Norway, a generation or so later, romanticism grew out of an enthusiastic study of popular ballads and folk-lore stories still found on the lips of the peasantry. In connection with this there developed an intense interest in rural scenery and life on the part of both artists and poets. The movement continued for a generation, until the early seventies, and found its best conscious literary expression in Björnson's peasant idyls. When Jonas Lie had resolved to become an author (1870), there was one region of romantic inspiration that had not been utilized. This was Nordland, one of the northerly provinces of Norway, beyond the Arctic Circle, under the glory of the midnight sun, where, however, a long and sunless winter fostered in the minds of the inhabitants a brooding melancholy which peopled mountain and sea, nature's every nook and cranny, with strange and awe-inspiring creatures. In this nature of colossal contrasts Jonas Lie spent several years of his boyhood, and the tremendous impression left on his sensitive and poetic mind are very evident in his first novel, *Second Sight* (*Den Fremsynte*), also known in English as *The Visionary* and *The Seer*. This, together with some lesser stories that followed, gave the Nordland stamp to Lie's earliest fiction—the stamp of romanticism, mysticism, and clairvoyance. The effect of this environment was accentuated by powerful innate impulses, for his ancestral heritage reveals a double strain, to which allusion has already been made. On his father's side there were, for several generations, brains, energy, and good sense, with a predilection for law and administration. The father himself was a country magistrate of sterling uprightness. Here, then, plainly enough, is the source of the novelist's realism, as found, for example, in *The Family at Gilje*, but nothing whatever to indicate the poet and romancer. These surely can be traced to the mother, who was a most remarkable woman, born in one of the northern provinces, and, as Lie himself believed, with either Finnish (*i.e.*, Lappic) or Gypsy blood in her veins, and possibly both. Professor Boyesen, in *Essays on Scandinavian Literature*, says of Lie's mother: "I remember well this black-eyed, eccentric little lady, with her queer ways and still more extraordinary conversation. It is from her that Jonas Lie has inherited the fantastic strain in his blood, the strange superstitious terrors, and the luxuriant wealth of color which he lavished upon his first novel, *The Man of Second Sight*. She was unusually gifted intellectually, had pronounced literary interests, and revealed some decided clairvoyant qualities." Lie himself said of her: "There was something of a seer in her—something that reminded one of spae-women and the like." "Imagine," says Arne Garborg,[1] in his book on Lie, "this restless blood infused into the strong, sober, practical nature of the Lies: what should come of such a mixture but that peculiar combination of reality and romanticism that we know by the name

---

[1] Arne Garborg is one of Norway's greatest novelists. He is also a gifted lyric poet, and an exceedingly clever controversialist. Most of his works are written in *Landsmaal*, a composite of the peasant dialects. His biography of Lie is a classic.

of Jonas Lie, the poet of Finnish magic and sorcery—and of plain reality." In Nordland, where his maternal inheritance had its source, Lie as a boy found things fit to satisfy the cravings of such an imagination as the Finn in him possessed. In this Brobdingnagian realm he heard tales and legends of Finnish sorcery, of shipwrecks caused by fierce water-bogies (*draugs*), of giant trolls, and a thousand other demoniacal creatures of morbid popular fancy, until he was chilled with terror, the effects of which clung to him for life, made him as a mature man afraid of the dark, and finally cropped out in tales of weird and grotesque imagery.

These, then, are the fundamental facts that are necessary for comprehension of the duality in Lie's nature and authorship.

Jonas Lie was born in southern Norway, in 1833, and at the age of five removed with the family to Nordland. His life as an author began in 1870; but between these dates there was a period of very unusual experiences. His vivid imagination, stirred by the witchery of life in Nordland, made the prosy tasks of school seem direst punishment. He was counted a dullard and an incorrigible mischief-maker. At the age of thirteen it was his passion to become a sailor. The father, at his wits' end, compromised by sending him to a naval academy. Here he was at times thought mad by his instructors, who saw something of his semi-somnambulistic antics. Near-sightedness, however, proved an obstacle to his continuance in *this* path to maritime glory, which he was destined to win by a different route. After an awakening experience in a Bergen school, where an eccentric poet-pedagogue thought him a "lad of pairts," and his classmates voted him a prize liar on account of his Nordland stories, he took a short cut to the university at Heltberg's so-called Student Factory in Christiania, the head-master of which—a prodigy who has been immortalized in literature by both Björnson and Garborg—proved an inspiring and fructifying force to his groping genius. At this institution, among a motley horde of country bumpkins, shipwrecked city talent, and budding genius, he found Björnson, also preparing for the university. Both were profoundly impressed by the genius of the asthmatic head-master in his dogskin jacket, who led his young barbarians by forced marches through the Alpine passes of Latin syntax into the classic domain of Livy and Horace. We shall see that he came to Lie's rescue at a later period.

Lie entered the university in 1851, and took a degree in law in 1858. It had been a difficult task for him to decide what professional study to pursue. He thought at first that he had leanings toward theology, bought the necessary books, kept them a day, then exchanged them for law books, after having paid a brief but adequate visit to the clinical laboratory. These years at the university, when a romantic interest in everything Norwegian filled the air with mystic expectancy of great things to come in the way of a regenerated Norway, aroused Lie. Association with Björnson, Ibsen, Vinje,[1] Nordraak,[2] and a score of other gifted young men was stimulating, yet he did not become a disciple or slavish follower of any of these more vehement natures. He had his own ideas, and was boldly independent when occasion demanded it, as both King Oscar and Björnson later in life ascertained to their discomfort, each of them having tried in vain to make the "amiable" author conform to their plans and ideas. Among the many friends that Lie made in the capital city during his university days, Björnson became the most intimate. He seems from the very first to have espied the artist in Lie, and did

---

[1] A peasant poet, kindred in spirit to both Burns and Heine.
[2] The composer of, among other notable things, the melody to Björnson's well-known national song. Before his death, at the age of twenty-four, he had given Edvard Grieg an electric spark from the dynamo of his Norse enthusiasm, which fired Grieg's imagination, and made him *par excellence* the representative of Norse melody.

much to help him in understanding his own strange self. It had begun to worry Lie that his friends thought him eccentric. And not only this: the mystic, superstitious, magic-loving Finn in his nature often frightened him. Hence he made great efforts to counteract his tendency to fantastic musing and to develop his paternal heritage: the rationalist and realist in himself. For this purpose the determination to study law was doubtless a wise step. But his legal studies did not suppress his literary yearnings, which found expression in verse that did not at first go beyond a circle of intimate friends. He saw no prospect of making a living with his pen, and so entered a government office — a decision hastily made under pressure of respect for his stern and practical father, who had announced a visit to the capital city. Nevertheless, he dreamed of becoming an author, and began contributing poems to the daily press. They seemed labored and heavy, and attracted no particular attention. On the other hand, he prepared some well-written articles on European politics, which indicated insight and careful thinking. These articles made such a favorable impression on Björnson that he offered to secure him the editorship of a Christiania daily. But Lie was unwilling. He had made arrangements to practise law at Kongsvinger, not far from the capital. After a year's work in the new field, he married a cousin, Thomasine Lie, to whom he had long been betrothed. Together they had planned that he was to be an author, and his hasty decision to become a lawyer was a severe shock to her. From the beginning she had faith in his literary possibilities; and it was evidently her steady hand on the rudder, throughout a long life, that guided the bark of his genius through many dangerous reefs. But for her good sense and loving loyalty, there would probably not have been a Jonas Lie in Norwegian literature. He often remarked that her name might well appear on the title-page of most of his books. In this most interesting partnership, his was the creative spirit, hers the practical guiding hand.

Lie's new home was in the heart of a rich timber district, which at that time was at the high tide of a tremendous business boom. Here he achieved immediate success as a lawyer. Moreover, through an influential friend, he became the financial agent of two banking houses in the capital. This gave him the opportunity—and he had the necessary courage—to take a hand in bold business enterprises on a large scale. He prospered; the future seemed roseate; he began to dream of such affluence as to enable him to devote himself to literature. Meanwhile he wrote verses for all manner of occasions, and even published a volume of these poems (1866). Both he and his wife had unusual social qualifications. She was a fine musician, a woman of character and much intellectual force, and a most competent housewife. In this home of culture many prominent men were entertained—first of all, Ole Bull, whom Lie adored. Mighty schemes for the glorification of Mother Norway were discussed as these two "visionaries" sat brewing their toddy. Björnson, too, was often there, and Sverdrup, the statesman.

Meanwhile clouds ominous of disaster appeared on the commercial horizon. The period 1865–68 witnessed the greatest financial panic that Norway had ever experienced. Lie had forebodings of a catastrophe, but too late to save himself. He had been lavish with his signature, and was tremendously involved. The crash meant more than life and death to him. It was a matter of honor, integrity, conscience. He lost everything, and was in debt to the extent of over $200,000. Lie, the lawyer, was ruined. He resolved to return to literature, for instinct urged him with "almost explosive force," to use his own phrase. As for his financial obligations, he made a monumental resolution, as did Walter Scott in a similar predicament, to pay every dollar through his authorship; and for years he dropped every penny that he did not absolutely need into that abyss of debt. Friends finally convinced him of the hopelessness of his purpose. With what a heavy heart Lie carried the tale of his bankruptcy to his faithful wife several of his novels testify. Financial crashes play no small part in his writings, and the pathetic force with which these situations are handled sounds a distinctly personal note.

With wife and children Lie returned to Christiania in the autumn of 1868—empty-handed. How he managed to keep his head above water by the aid of loyal friends like Björnson, Sverdrup, whose private secretary he was for a time, and old Heltberg, of the Student Factory, who came to engage him as a teacher of rhetoric and composition, is an interesting story which need not be told here. But through all his trials one determination was fixed and inflexible: he would make literature his life-work. It was not long before his thoughts reverted to his early experiences in Nordland. After several years of subjection to the stern reality of legal and commercial enterprise, the Finn was again asserting himself. His first novel, *Second Sight*, was the result. He read it to his wife; she thought it magnificent, but later applied the pruning-knife drastically. Then Björnson was called in. He concurred in the wife's opinion, and immediately wrote the great Copenhagen publisher, Hegel, pronouncing the novel a "sea-mew" that would fly over all the Scandinavian North, and urging hasty publication. This was in November, 1870. By Christmas the book was in the shops. In large part it purports to be the autobiography of a visionary Nordlander, who tells of his beloved home, and recounts marvellous stories of the Arctic north; but through this bead-string of episodes and descriptions there is interwoven a pathetic tale of love, love so tender, so delicate, that the words describing it seem to come tripping on tiptoe. Unpromising as the novel seems in the beginning, when one almost expects a study in the pathology of second sight, it nevertheless develops into such beauty as to make it the *Romeo and Juliet* of Scandinavian literature.

Every step of Jonas Lie's development from this first novel to *The Family at Gilje* (1883) is of interest to the student of literature. It was a period of hard study, careful, conscientious work, and high resolve to master his powers and to utilize his varied experiences for literary purposes, in order to be able to serve Mother Norway,—for one must never forget the intense patriotic ardor of all Norway's great writers, artists, and musicians. By the aid of a government stipend, Lie was enabled to visit Nordland and the western coast to promote his literary production, and soon afterward a second and larger stipend for the purpose of foreign travel made it possible for him to visit Rome, the Mecca of all Scandinavian artists and *literati* of the period. There he remained more than three years, a time of fruitful toil and stimulating experience. In 1872 he sent home two books relating to life on the western and northern coast, *The Good Ship Future*, and a collection of short stories.

Lie was not content, however, to be "the poet of Nordland," as he at once had been named. His ambition was to be more national. In the broader realms of literary activity the giant figures of Ibsen and Björnson towered. They were deep in the problems of the day. How could he become national and modern? Instinct led him on in paths that unconsciously he had already trodden. In this nation of seafarers he was the first in modern literature to discover the coast-dwellers and to portray their struggles on the sea. His first book contained a description of a storm in northern waters that makes the reader hold his breath. In the volume of short stories, which in their scenes sweep along the western coast, and in *The Good Ship Future* as well, there was a distinct odor of the sea. This was natural enough: he had spent his early years in Nordland and in Bergen, the centre of Norwegian shipping, and he loved the sea passionately. In his next novel, *The Pilot and his Wife*, he put to sea with sails hoisted to the top.

The critics apparently had not felt the sea-breezes in his first books; but in the last there blew such a lusty gale that all, both critics and public, sniffed its fresh and salty breath with keenest relish. The book was a success, which his previous novel had not quite been, and it marks the beginning of Lie's sane and natural realism as consciously applied, in its main problem, to a modern social question, making the story, in its essence, a novel of character, a psychological study of the relation of man and wife, and not primarily a novel of adventure, which assumption gave Lie the designation "novelist of the sea." The success of the book brought the author, in 1874, by vote of the Storting, a life stipend known as a "poet's salary," which recognition put him in a class with Ibsen and Björnson. The great honor seems to have had a depressing effect, for Lie now scored four failures in succession. He was back in Norway, trying to portray social phenomena of the capital city. The reviewers were most irritating and offensive, and he felt obliged temporarily to desert the field. With the novel *Rutland* (1881), he returned to the sea. This story surpasses *The Pilot* in every respect. The sea is described with the fondness of a lover. Like *The Pilot*, it also deals with a problem of the home, but what chiefly impressed the public in reading the book was that the seamen, that important element of the Norwegian people, had found an adequate interpreter.

His next book, *Forward* (*Gaa Paa*) (1882), was likewise a maritime novel, with panoramas in the life of the fisher folk on the western coast. At the same time it forecast the new age of industrial development, and revealed growing sympathy and increased understanding in matters of national import. The author seems to have become convinced that a novelist, too, might be able to lend a hand in paving the way for progress. In this book he had by his vivid portrayal attacked stagnation, superstition, sluggishness, and had proclaimed the new gospel of work, activity, enterprise. It had been begun during the latter part of a three years' sojourn in Germany. It was completed in Norway during the autumn of 1882, after which Lie took up his abode in Paris, where he made his home for many years.

For his next work, *A Life Prisoner* (1883), Lie found his theme in the slums of Christiania. The treatment was not naturalistic enough to satisfy the critics. Lie was of course not unmindful of the new literary movement, but he possessed then, as always, sufficient individual momentum to carry him through the ephemeral phases of literary fads. His novels are not barometers of the prevailing literary atmosphere. He believed in a realism of true naturalism, which has stood the test of time. In this last work he brings a waif of modern society close to the hearts of his readers, and needs no explosions of pent-up indignation, no spirit of class hatred, to make his readers understand this unfortunate product of a bad environment. In his reply to the critics, Lie spoke forcibly on the new literary method, summing up his views in these words: "The main thing is to picture life so that the reader sees, hears, feels, comprehends it; by what esthetic means this is accomplished must be the author's own affair in each individual case. But experience has shown that of all methods direct ones are often the least effective. A single deft touch may save a dozen pages of detailed description." Lie was not a student of the base; he did not even have an artistic liking for evil. There are few bad characters in his works.

It was immediately after his controversy with the critics, in 1883, that *The Family at Gilje* appeared — a superb illustration of Lie's realism of naturalness. An American critic has said of good realistic writing that it does not so much arouse the pleasure of surprise as that of recognition. To intelligent Norwegian readers of the day that was strikingly true of

The Family at Gilje. To many readers it seemed like living their lives over again. This may not be a very severe test of the greatness of a novel. Greatness will depend upon other things — the breadth and depth of its humanity. Another point: "The right understanding of men and women leads to the right relations of men and women, and in this way a novel may do good" (F. Marion Crawford). Most of Lie's novels seem to have been written with this object in view. It is evident that in an attempt to portray life for this purpose, social and other questions are sure to appear — not thrust into the reader's face as a problem demanding that he take sides, but brought to his attention naturally, as such things ordinarily come in life. Discreetly done, as Lie surely could do it, this may be a most effective way of revolutionizing conscience. In this artistic manner Lie was, and no doubt consciously, a reformer. To be sure, this is not art for art's sake; it is something more human: art engaged in the pursuit of stimulating noble and healthful thought for the purpose of raising the average of human happiness.

It was this calm and restrained realistic method that Lie now applied in a series of novels which succeeded *The Family at Gilje*. As in this work, the scenes are usually laid in a preceding generation, preferably among the official class in the country.

In these homes, which Lie knew so well, we feel that we are with real and natural people among whom problems are not discussed, but experienced. Yet these novels were not so conservative as they seemed. They had persuasive power in behalf of modern ideas with respect to such fundamental things as marriage, home, and children. There was even something of the essence of social dynamite in some of them. *The Family at Gilje* gave the champions of women new arguments, but they could not approve of the author's advanced sympathies in *The Commodore's Daughters*, one of the realistic novels which now flowed from Lie's pen and which included: *A Maelstrom* (1884), *The Commodore's Daughters* (1885), *A Wedded Life* (1887), *Maisa Jons* (1888), and *Evil Powers* (1890). Suddenly there came a change in his literary method, seemingly induced by some unpleasant experience with good friends. He had learned that the conduct of the best of men is often swayed by primal instinct rather than by disciplined reason. In this mood he reverted to the trusty Finn of his bosom who so long had lain dormant, and let him discourse on life and human nature. He proved voluble, resourceful, and original. The result was published in two volumes (1891 and 1892), entitled *Trold*. They are, in part, phantasmagorias charged with the symbolism of Norse legendary lore, where trolls are the personified manifestation of evil forces in nature. The opening sentence of the illuminating introduction says: "That there are trolls in human beings every one knows who has an eye for that sort of thing."

In the most characteristic of these stories, of which there are a dozen in each volume, Lie has personified primal instincts, — allegorized some of the strange facts and mystic forces of nature, man, and society. Others are in lighter vein and have a more human cast, being mere playful satires on social phenomena. They form a marvellous medley. At first it seems quite impossible to believe that the author of *The Family at Gilje* can be the begetter of things so fantastic and grotesque. But when the reader thinks of the early Nordland stories, he understands, and then feels inclined to regret, that the Finn had so long lain dormant. One is tempted to believe that a little of the troll element could easily have been used to give a tinge of terror to his calm realism; and this is in fact what he has done most effectively in the novel *Dyre Rein* (1896), which in other respects much resembles *The Family at Gilje*.

After the publication of *Trold*, Lie, even where he does not introduce troll effects, is not hesitant about using more tragic methods and more dramatic scenes than during the period of the strictly realistic novels. There is, moreover, a decided trend toward a wider scope and more cosmopolitan aims, as in *When the Iron Curtain Falls* (1901), a bolder symbolism, as in *Niobe* (1893) and in his last work, *East of the Sun, West of the Moon, and Beyond the Towers of Babylon* (1905), in which, however, as the title indicates, the story is top-heavy with symbolism. It runs parallel with the main narrative as an introduction to each chapter. The whole is the tale of a genius, hampered and harassed by malicious trolls in human guise—evidently an adumbration of the author's own personal experience. But he is, as always, charitable: "Human nature is so complex!"

In other words: the last fifteen years of Lie's authorship reveal him in full possession of the realistic powers of the preceding period, illuminated by a profound comprehension of the mystic forces of life that so often determine human fates.

Like Ibsen, Lie lived abroad for many years, mainly in Paris, but usually spending his summers in the Bavarian Alps, where most of his writing was done. There were too many distractions in Paris, where his home was a centre of the colony of Scandinavian artists and literary workers. In the summer of 1893, after an absence of ten years, he felt the need of visiting Norway again. An intense feeling of homesickness had seized him, as the following incident will indicate. He had called on a Norwegian family in Paris who had just received a plant from Norway in Norwegian earth. "Thinking himself unobserved," one of his daughters tells, "I saw him turn from the company, take a pinch of that earth and put it to his mouth. Whether he kissed it or ate it I do not know. But he looked very solemn."

In Norway he was received most cordially. On the occasion of his sixtieth birthday, Brandes proclaimed him "the most amiable of geniuses." He was interviewed, banqueted, and serenaded almost to distraction, and was glad to get back to Paris, happy, however, in having experienced the touching devotion of his countrymen. A decade of arduous toil followed, after which he began to make plans for returning to Norway to spend the last years of his life. A cozy home was built at Fredriksværn, on the southern coast, and in 1906 the family took possession of it. The next year, however, his faithful wife, the guardian of his genius, passed away. Dependent upon her companionship and solicitous care, he did not long survive her. He died July 5, 1908.

The Norwegian Storting took fitting cognizance

of his death, and, as had been done at Ibsen's demise, decreed that interment should be made at the expense of the State.

"Blessed are the merciful," said the pastor at his bier.

"Be merciful!" is the sentiment that echoes and reëchoes throughout Jonas Lie's pages.

JULIUS E. OLSON

The University of Wisconsin
  February, 1920

THE FAMILY AT GILJE

THE FAMILY AT GILJE

Chapter I

IT was a clear, cold afternoon in the mountain region. The air lay blue with the frost, with light rose tints over all the sharp crests, ravines, and peaks, which, like a series of gigantic drifts, tower above tower, floated up towards the horizon. Below, hills and wooded mountain slopes shut the region in with white walls, constantly narrower and narrower, nearer and nearer, always more contracting.

The snow was late this year, but in return, now that the Christmas season had come, lay so heavy on fir and spruce that it bent down both needles and twigs. The groves of birches stood up to their waists in snow; the small clusters of tile-roofed houses of the district were half buried, with snow-drifts pressing down over the roofs. The entrances to the farmyards were deeply dug paths, from which the gate and fence posts stuck up here and there like the masts of sunken boats.

The snow-plough had recently gone through the highway, and on the steep red-tiled roof of the captain's house men were busy shovelling down the great frozen snow-drifts, which hung threatening over the ends of the roof.

The captain's house was specially prominent in

the district. It was unpainted and built of square logs, like the greater part of that kind of houses a generation ago.

Over the garden fence and almost up under the window-frames lay the snow-drifts with tracks of sleds and skis in their icy crust, which smoked a little in the frosty north wind under the sun.

It was the same cold, disagreeable north wind which, every time the outer door was opened, blew against the kitchen door until that opened too, and, if it was not closed again, soon after, one or another door on the next floor,—and that made the captain come down from his office, flushed and passionate, to make inquiries and fret and fume over the whole house as to who had gone there first and who had gone last. He could never understand why they did not keep the door shut, though the matter was most easily to be understood,—for the latch was old and loose, and the captain would never spend any money on the smith for a new one.

In the common room below, between the sofa and the stove, the captain's wife, in an old brown linsey-woolsey dress, sat sewing. She had a tall, stiff figure, and a strong, but gaunt, dried-up face, and had the appearance of being anxiously occupied at present by an intricate problem — the possibility of again being able to put a new durable patch on the seat of Jörgen's trousers; they were always bottomless — almost to desperation.

CHAPTER I

She had just seized the opportunity for this, while Jäger was up in his office, and the children were gone to the post-office; for she went about all day long like a horse grinding clay in a brickyard.

The mahogany sewing-table inlaid with mother-of-pearl and several different kinds of wood, which stood open before her, must have been a family heirloom; in its condition of faded antiquity, it reminded one not a little of her, and in any event did not at all correspond either with the high-backed, rickety, leather armchair, studded with brass nails, in which she sat, nor with the long birchen sofa covered with green linsey-woolsey, which stood like a solitary deserted land against the wall, and seemed to look longingly over to the brown, narrow folding-table, which, with its leaves let down, stood equally solitary and abandoned between the two windows.

The brown case with the four straight legs against the farther wall, with a heap of papers, books, hats, and the spy-glass upon it, was an old clavichord, which, with great trouble, she had had transported up into the mountain region, out of the effects of her home, and on which she had faithfully practised with her children the same pieces which she herself had learned.

The immense every-day room, with the bare timber walls, the unpainted sanded floor, and the small panes with short curtains fastened up in the middle, was in its whole extent extremely scantily furnished; it was half a mile from chair to chair, and everything had a rural meagreness such as one could often see in the homes of officials in the mountain districts in the forties. In the middle of the inner wall, before the great white fire-wall, the antique stove with the Naes iron-works stamp and the knotty wooden logs under it jutted out into the room like a mighty giant. Indeed, nothing less than such a mass of iron was needed to succeed in warming up the room; and in the woods of the captain's farm there was plenty of fuel.

Finally abandoning all more delicate expedients for the trousers, she had laid on a great patch covering everything, and was now sewing zealously. The afternoon sun was still shedding a pale yellow light in the window-frames; it was so still in the room that her movements in sewing were almost audible, and a spool of thread which fell down caused a kind of echo.

All at once she raised herself like a soldier at an order and gave attention. She heard her husband's quick, heavy step creaking on the stairs.

Was it the outside door again?

Captain Jäger, a red, round, and stout man in a threadbare uniform coat, came hastily in, puffing, with the still wet quill-pen in his mouth; he went straight to the window.

His wife merely sewed more rapidly; she wished

CHAPTER I

to use the time, and also prudently to assume the defensive against what might come.

He breathed on the frosty pane in order to enlarge the part that could be seen through. "You will see there is something by the mail. The children are running a race down there in the road,—they are running away from Jörgen with the sled."

The needle only flew still faster.

"Ah, how they run!—Thinka and Thea. But Inger-Johanna! Come here, Ma, and see how she puts down her feet—is n't it as if she was dancing? Now she means to be the first in, and so she will be the first, that I promise you. It is no story when I tell you that the lass is handsome, Ma; that they all see. Ah, come and look how she gets ahead of Thinka! Just come now, Ma!"

But "Ma" did not stir. The needle moved with forced nervous haste. The captain's wife was sewing a race with what was coming; it was even possible that she might get the last of the patch finished before they entered, and just now the sun disappeared behind the mountain crest; they were short days it gave them up there.

The steps outside were taken in two or three leaps, and the door flew open.

Quite right—Inger-Johanna.

She rushed in with her cloak unfastened and covered with snow. She had untied the strings of her hood on the way up the steps, so that her black hair fell down in confusion over her hot face. Breathless, she threw her flowered Valders mittens on a chair. She stood a moment to get her breath, brushed her hair under her hood, and shouted out:

"An order for post-horses at the station, for Captain Rönnow and Lieutenant Mein. The horses are to be here at Gilje at six o'clock to-morrow morning. They are coming here."

"Rönnow, Ma!" roared the captain, surprised; it was one of the comrades of his youth.

Now the others also came storming in with the details.

The mother's pale face, with its marked features and smooth black hair in loops down over her cheeks in front of her cap, assumed a somewhat thoughtful, anxious expression. Should the veal roast be sacrificed which she had reserved for the dean, or the pig? The latter had been bought from the north district, and was fearfully poor.

"Well, well, I bet he is going to Stockholm," continued the captain, meditatively drumming on the window-frame. "Adjutant, perhaps; they would not let that fellow stay out there in the West. Do you know, Ma, I have thought of something of this sort ever since the prince had so much to do with him at the drill-ground. I often said to him, 'Your stories, Rönnow, will make your fortune,— but look out for the general, he knows a thing or

CHAPTER I

two.' 'Pooh! that goes down like hot cakes,' said he. And it looks like it — the youngest captain!"

"The prince—" The captain's wife was just through with the trousers, and rose hastily. Her meagre, yellowish face, with its Roman nose, assumed a resolute expression: she decided on the fatted calf.

"Inger-Johanna, see to it that your father has his Sunday wig on," she exclaimed hurriedly, and hastened out into the kitchen.

The stove in the best room was soon packed full, and glowing. It had not been used since it had been rubbed up and polished with blacking last spring, and smoked now so that they were obliged to open door and windows to the cold, though it was below zero.

Great-Ola, the farm-hand, had been busy carrying large armfuls of long wood into the kitchen, and afterwards with brushing the captain's old uniform coat with snow out on the porch; it must not look as if he had dressed up.

The guest-chamber was made ready, with the beds turned down, and the fire started, so that the thin stove snapped, and the flies suddenly woke up and buzzed under the ceiling, while the wainscot was browned outside of the fire-wall and smelled of paint. Jörgen's hair was wet and combed; the girls changed their aprons to be ready to go down and greet the guests, and were set to work rolling up pipe-lighters for the card-table.

They kept looking out as long as the twilight lasted, both from the first and second story windows, while Great-Ola, with his red peaked cap, made a path in the snow to the carriage-road and the steps.

And now, when it was dark, the children listened with beating hearts for the slightest sound from the road. All their thoughts and longings went out towards the strange, distant world which so rarely visited them, but of which they heard so much that sounded grand and marvellous.

There are the bells!

But, no; Thinka was entirely wrong.

They had all agreed to that fact, when Inger-Johanna, who stood in the dark by a window which she held a little open, exclaimed, "But there they are!"

Quite right. They could hear the sleigh-bells, as the horse, moving by fits and starts, laboriously made his way up the Gilje hills.

The outside door was opened, and Great-Ola stood at the stairs, holding the stable lantern with a tallow candle in it, ready to receive them.

A little waiting, and the bells suddenly sounded plainly in the road behind the wood-shed. Now you could hear the snow creaking under the runners.

CHAPTER I

The captain placed the candlestick on the table in the hall, the floor of which had been freshly scoured, washed, and strewn with juniper. He went out on the stairs, while the children, head to head, peeped out of the kitchen door, and kept Pasop, who growled and fretted behind them, from rushing out and barking.

"Good-evening, Rönnow! Good-evening, Lieutenant! Welcome to Gilje!" said the captain with his strong, cheerful voice, while the vehicle, which at the last post-house was honored with the name of double sleigh, swung into the yard and up to the steps. "You are elegantly equipped, I see."

"Beastly cold, Peter,—beastly cold, Peter," came the answer from the tall figure wrapped in furs, as he threw down the reins, and, now a little stiff in his movements, stepped out of the sleigh, while the steaming horse shook himself in his harness so that the bells rang loudly. "I believe we are frozen stiff. And then this little rat we have for a horse would not go. It is a badger dog they have harnessed in order to dig our way through the snow-drifts. How are you, Peter? It will be pleasant to get into your house. How goes it?" he concluded, upon the steps, shaking the captain's hand. "Bring in the case of bottles, Lieutenant."

While the two gentlemen took off their furs and travelling-boots in the hall and paid for the horse, and Great-Ola carried the trunk up to the guest-chamber, an odor of incense diffused itself from the large room, which at once roused Captain Rönnow's cavalier instinct to a recollection of the lady, whom, in the joy of seeing his old comrade once more, he had forgotten. His large, stately figure stopped before the door, and he adjusted his stock.

"Do I look tolerably well, Peter, so I can properly appear before your wife?" he said, running his hand through his black curly hair.

"Yes, yes, fine enough — devilish fine-looking fellow, Lieutenant. — If you please, gentlemen. Captain Rönnow and Lieutenant Mein, Ma," he said, as he opened the door.

The mistress of the house rose from her place at the table, where she was now sitting with fine white knitting-work. She greeted Captain Rönnow as heartily as her stiff figure would allow, and the lieutenant somewhat critically. It was the governor's sister to whom the salaam was made, as Captain Rönnow afterwards expressed it — an old, great family.

She disappeared a little later into domestic affairs, to "get them something for supper."

Captain Rönnow rubbed his hands from the cold, wheeled around on one leg on the floor, and thus placed himself with his back to the stove. "I tell you we are frozen stiff, Peter, — but — Oh, Lieutenant, bring in the case of bottles."

When Lieutenant Mein came in again, Rönnow

took a sealed bottle with a label, and held it, swinging by the neck, before the captain.

"Look at it, Peter Jäger! Look well at it!" and he moved over towards his friend. "Genuine arrack from Atschin in hither—farther—East—or West India. I present it to you. May it melt your heart, Peter Jäger!"

"Hot water and sugar, Ma!" shouted the captain out into the kitchen, "then we shall soon know whether you only mean to deceive us simple country folks with stories. And out with the whist-table till we have supper! We can play three-handed whist with a dummy."

"Brrr-rr-whew, what kind of stuff is it you've got in your tobacco box, Jäger?" said Captain Rönnow, who was filling his pipe at it; "powder, sneezing powder, I believe! Smell it, Lieutenant. It must be tansy from the nursery."

"Tideman's three crown, fellow! We can't endure your leaf tobacco and Virginia up here in the mountain districts," came from Jäger, who was pulling out and opening the card-table. "Only look at the next box under the lead cover, and you will find some cut-leaf tobacco, Bremen leaf, as black and high flavored as you want. Up here it is only to the goats that we can offer that kind, and to the folk who come from Bergen; they use strong tobacco there to dry out the wet fog."

The door opened, and the three girls and their

little brother came in, carrying the tray with the glasses and the jug of hot water, which task they seemed to have apportioned among themselves according to the rules for the procession at the Duke of Marlborough's funeral, where, as is known, the fourth one carried nothing.

The tall, blond Kathinka marched at the head with the tray and glasses with the clinking teaspoons in them. She attempted the feat of curtseying, while she was carrying the tray, and blushed red when it was ready to slip, and the lieutenant was obliged to take hold of it to steady it.

He immediately noticed the next oldest, a brunette with long eyelashes, who was coming with the smoking water-jug on a plate, while the youngest, Thea, was immediately behind her with the sugar-bowl.

"But, my dear Peter Jäger," exclaimed Rönnow, astonished at the appearance of his friend's almost grown-up daughters, "when have you picked up all this? You wrote once about some girls,—and a boy who was to be baptized."

At the same moment Jörgen came boldly forward, strutting over the floor, and made his best bow, while he pulled his bristly yellow locks instead of his cap.

"What is your name?"

"Jörgen Winnecken von Zittow Jäger."

"That was heavy! You are a perfect mountain

boy, are you not? Let me see you kick as high as your name."

"No, but as high as my cap," answered Jörgen, going back on the floor and turning a cart-wheel.

"Bold fellow, that Jörgen!" And with that, as Jörgen had done his part, he stepped back into obscurity. But while the gentlemen were pouring out the arrack punch at the folding-table, he kept his eyes uninterruptedly fastened on Lieutenant Mein. It was the lieutenant's regularly trimmed black moustache, which seemed to him like bits that he had not got into his mouth properly.

"Oh, here, my girl!" said Rönnow, turning to one of the daughters, who stood by his side while he was putting some sugar into the steaming glass, "what is your name?"

"Inger-Johanna."

"Yes, listen"—he spoke without seeing anything else than the arm he touched to call her attention. "Listen, my little Inger-Johanna! In the breast pocket of my fur coat out in the hall there are two lemons—I didn't believe that fruit grew up here in the mountains, Peter!—two lemons."

"No, let me! Pardon me!" and the lieutenant flew gallantly.

Captain Rönnow looked up, astonished. The dark, thin girl, in the outgrown dress which hung about her legs, and the three thick, heavy, black cables, braided closely for the occasion, hanging down her back, stood distinct in the light before him. Her neck rose, delicately shaped and dazzlingly fresh, from the blue, slightly low-cut, linsey-woolsey dress, and carried her head proudly, with a sort of swan-like curve.

The captain grasped at once why the lieutenant was so alert.

"Bombs and grenades, Peter!" he exclaimed.

"Do you hear that, Ma?" the captain grunted slyly.

"Up here among the peasants the children—more's the pity—grow up without any other manners than those that they learn of the servants," sighed the mother. "Don't stand so bent over, Thinka, straighten up."

Thinka straightened up her overgrown blond figure and tried to smile. She had the difficult task of hiding a plaster on one side of her chin, where a day or two before she had fallen down through the cellar trap-door in the kitchen.

Soon the three gentlemen sat comfortably at their cards, each one smoking his pipe and with a glass of hot arrack punch by his side. Two moulded tallow candles in tall brass candlesticks stood on the card-table and two on the folding-table; they illuminated just enough so that you could see the almanac, which hung down by a piece of twine from a nail under the looking-glass, and a part of the lady's tall form and countenance, while she sat knitting in her frilled cap. In the darkness of the room the chairs farthest off by the stove could hardly be distinguished from the kitchen door—from which now and then came the hissing of the roasting meat.

"Three tricks, as true as I live—three tricks, and by those cards!" exclaimed Captain Rönnow, eager in the game.

"Thanks, thanks," turning to Inger-Johanna who brought a lighted paper-lighter to his expiring pipe. "Th-a-nks"—he continued, drawing in the smoke and puffing it out, his observant eyes again being attracted by her. Her expression was so bright, the great dark eyes moving to and fro under her eyebrows like dark drops, while she stood following the cards.

"What is your name, once more, my girl?" he asked absently.

"Inger-Johanna," she replied with a certain humor; she avoided looking at him.

"Yes, yes.—Now it is my turn to deal! Your daughter puts a bee in my bonnet, madam. I should like to take her with me to Christiania to the governor's, and bring her out. We would make a tremendous sensation, that I am sure of."

"At last properly dealt! Play."

With her hands on the back of her father's chair, Inger-Johanna gazed intently on the cards; but her face had a heightened glow.

Rönnow glanced at her from one side. "A sight

for the gods, a sight for the gods!" he exclaimed, as he gathered together with his right hand the cards he had just arranged, and threw them on the table. "Naturally I mean how the lieutenant manages dummy — you understand, madam," nodding to her with significance. "Heavens! Peter, that was a card to play.— Here you can see what I mean," he continued. "Trump, trump, trump, trump!" He eagerly threw four good spades on the table, one after another, without paying any attention to what followed.

The expression of the lady's face, as she sat there and heard her innermost thoughts repeated so plainly, was immovably sealed; she said, somewhat indifferently, "It is high time, children, you said good-night; it is past your bed-time. Say good-night to the gentlemen."

The command brought disappointment to their faces; not obeying was out of the question, and they went round the table, and made curtsies and shook hands with the captain and the lieutenant.

The last thing Jörgen noticed was that the lieutenant turned round, stretched his neck, and gaped like Svarten as they went out.

Their mother straightened up over her knitting-work. "You used to visit my brother's, the governor's, formerly, Captain Rönnow," she ventured. "They are childless folk, who keep a hospitable house. You will call on them now, I suppose."

CHAPTER I

"Certainly I shall! To refrain from doing that would be a crime! You have, I should imagine, thought of sending one of your daughters there. The governor's wife is a person who knows how to introduce a young lady into the world, and your Inger-Johanna—"

The captain's wife answered slowly and with some stress; something of a suppressed bitterness rose up in her. "That would be an entirely unexpected piece of good fortune; but more than we out-of-the-way country folk can expect of our grand, distinguished sister-in-law. Small circumstances make small folk, more's the pity; large ones ought to make them otherwise.—My brother has made her a happy wife."

"Done. Will you allow an old friend to work a little for your attractive little Inger?" returned Captain Rönnow.

"I think that Ma will thank you. What do you say, Gitta? Then you will have a peg to hang one of them on. It can't be from one of us two that Inger-Johanna has inherited her beauty, Ma!" said Captain Jäger, coughing and warding off his wife's admonitory look; "but there is blood, both on her father's and mother's side. Her great-grandmother was married off up in Norway by the Danish queen because she was too handsome to be at court—it was your grandmother, Ma! Fröken von—"

"My dear Jäger," begged his wife.

"Pshaw, Ma! The sand of many years has been strewed over that event."

When the game was again started, the captain's wife went with her knitting-work to the card-table, snuffed first one candle and then the other, leaned over her husband, and whispered something.

The captain looked up, rather surprised. "Yes, indeed, Ma! Yes, indeed—'My camel for your dromedary,' said Peter Vangensten, when he swapped his old spavined horse for Mamen's blooded foal. If you come with your arrack from Holland and farther India, then I put my red wine direct from France against it—genuine Bordeaux, brought home and drawn straight from the hogshead! There were just two dozen the governor sent us with the wagon the autumn Jörgen was baptized. —The two farthest to the left, Ma! You had better take Marit with you with the lantern. Then you can tell the governor's wife that we drank her health up here among the snow-drifts, Rönnow."

"Yes, she is very susceptible to that kind of thing, Peter Jäger."

When the captain's wife came in again, she had the stiff damask tablecloth on her arm, and was accompanied by a girl who helped move the folding-table out on the floor. It was to be set for supper, and the card-table must be moved into the best room, across the hall, which was now warm.

"Can you wait, Ma, till the rubber is played?"

CHAPTER I

Ma did not answer; but they felt the full pressure of her silence; her honor was at stake—the roast veal.

And they played on silently, but at a tearing pace as with full steam.

Finally the captain exclaimed, while Ma stood immovable with the cloth in the middle of the floor, "There, there, we must get away, Rönnow!"

In the chamber above, impatient hearts were hammering and beating.

While Jörgen went to sleep with the image before him of his lieutenant who gaped like Svarten when he came out of the stable door into the light, and after Torbjörg had put out the candle, the sisters stole out into the great, cold, dark hall. There they all three stood, leaning over the balustrade, and gazing down on the fur coats and mufflers, which hung on the timber wall, and on the whip and the two sabre sheaths and the case of bottles, which were dimly lighted by the stable lantern on the hall table.

They smelt the odor of the roast as it came up, warm and appetizing, and saw when the guests, each with his punch-glass in his hand and with flickering candle, went across the hall into the large room. They heard the folding-table moved out and set, and later caught the sound of the clinking of glasses, laughter, and loud voices.

Every sound from below was given a meaning, every fragment of speech was converted into a romance for their thirsty fancy.

They stood there in the cold till their teeth chattered and their limbs shook against the wood-work, so that they were obliged to get into bed again to thaw out.

They heard how the chairs made a noise when the guests rose from the table, and they went out in the hall again, Thinka and Inger-Johanna,—Thea was asleep. It helped a little when they put their feet upon the lowest rail of the balustrade, or hung over it with their legs bent double under them.

Thinka held out because Inger-Johanna held out; but finally she was compelled to give up, she could not feel her legs any more. And now Inger-Johanna alone hung down over the balustrade.

A sort of close odor of punch and tobacco smoke frozen together rose up through the stairs in the cold, and every time the door was opened and showed the heavy, smoky, blue gleam of light in the great room, she could hear officers' names, fragments of laughter, of violent positive assertions, with profane imprecations by all possible and impossible powers of the heavens above and the earth beneath, and between them her father's gay voice, —all chopped off in mince-meat every time the door was shut.

When Inger-Johanna went to bed again, she lay

CHAPTER I

thinking how Captain Rönnow had asked her twice what her name was, and then again how at the card-table he had said, "I should like to take her with me to the governor's wife; we would make a tremendous sensation." And then what came next, "Naturally I mean how the lieutenant plays dummy,"—which they thought she did not understand.

The wind blew and howled around the corner of the house, and whistled down through the great plastered chimney-pipe in the hall—and she still, half in her dreams, heard Captain Rönnow's "Trump! trump! trump! trump!"

The next day Ma went about the house as usual with her bunch of keys; she had hardly slept at all that night.

She had become old before her time, like so many other "mas," in the household affairs of that period—old by bearing petty annoyances, by toil and trouble, by never having money enough, by bending and bowing, by continually looking like nothing and being everything—the one on whom the whole anxious care of the house weighed.

But—"One lives for the children."

That was Ma's pet sigh of consolation. And the new time had not yet come to the "mas" with the question whether they were not also bound to realize their own personal lives.

But for the children it was a holiday, and immediately after breakfast they darted into the great room.

There stood the card-table, again moved against the wall, with the cards thrown in a disorderly pile over the paper on which the score had been kept. It had been folded up and burned on one end for a lighter; and by its side, during a preliminary cleaning, the three pipes were lying, shoved aside. One window was still open, notwithstanding the wind blew in so that the fastening hook rattled.

There was something in the room — a pungent odor, which was not good; no, but there was, nevertheless, something about it — something of an actual occurrence.

Outside of the window Great-Ola stood with his hands on the shovel in the steep snow-drift, listening to Marit's account of how the captain had left a broad two-kroner piece for drink money on the table up in the guest-chamber and the lieutenant a shilling under the candlestick, and how the mistress had divided them among the girls.

"The lieutenant was not so butter-fingered," suggested Marit.

"Don't you know that a lieutenant would be shot if he gave as much as his captain, girl," retorted Great-Ola, while she hurried in with the keys of the storehouse and the meal-chest.

From the captain's sleeping-room the sound of his snoring could be heard for the whole forenoon.

CHAPTER I

The guests did not go to bed, and started at six o'clock in the morning, when the post-boy came to the door—after the second bottle, also, of Rönnow's Indian arrack had been emptied, and a breakfast with whiskey, brawn, and the remnants of the roast veal had strengthened them for the day's journey.

But the thing to be done was to have a good time on the holiday. The sisters bustled about in the hall with their skis, and Jörgen was trying how the outer steps would do for a ski slide.

Soon they were out on the long steep hill behind the cow-barn—the ski-staff in both hands in front for a balance, their comforters streaming out behind their necks. In the jump Inger-Johanna lost her balance and almost—no, she kept up!

It was because she looked up to the window of the sleeping-room to see if her father appreciated her skill.

He was walking about and dressing. Ma had at last, about dinner time, ventured to wake him up.

Chapter II

TWO days before Christmas Great-Ola with Svarten and his load was expected from Christiania, where he went twice a year, St. John's Day and Christmas, for the household supplies. To-day was the ninth day; but in sleighing like this, when the horse's feet struck through at every step, no one could be sure of anything.

The load, met on the run, far down the slippery, slushy hill, by the children and the barking, one-eyed Pasop, came along in the afternoon, while Svarten, even in his exertions on the steep part of the hill, neighed and whinnied with pleasure at being home again and longing to get into the stall by the side of Brunen. He had had quite enough of the journey, and worked himself into a foam in the harness to get over the Gilje hill.

Marit, the cook, and Torbjörg were out in the porch before the kitchen; the three girls and Jörgen stood wholly absorbed by the load and the horse, and the captain himself came down the stairs.

"Well, Great-Ola, how has Svarten pulled through? Sweaty and tired, I see! Did you get my uniform buttons? Ah, well! I hope you did not forget the tobacco!—And my watch, could they do anything with that?—Have you the bill?—Well, then, you must put up Svarten—he shall have an extra feed of oats to-day. What? What have you got there?"

Besides the bill, Great-Ola had taken out of his inside vest pocket a letter wrapped up in paper, blue postal paper, with a beautiful red seal on it. The captain looked at it a moment with surprise. It was the writing of the governor's wife and her seal in the wax, and without saying a word he hastened in to his wife.

The load from the city, the great event of the half year, occupied the attention of the whole household. Its contents interested all, not the children alone, and when Great-Ola, later in the evening, sat in the kitchen, where he was treated as a guest on account of his return home, and told about his trip to the city and about Svarten and himself, what miracles they had wrought on such and such hills—and the load weighed this time at least two hundred pounds more than the last—then there was a sort of glamor about him and Svarten, too.

One evening he had even found his way in a snowstorm, and once the salt-bag was forgotten, and then Svarten actually would not stir from the inn-yard, but lashed his tail at every cut of the whip, and kept looking back, until the boy came running out of the hall and shouted out about the bag, then off he started willingly enough.

The captain had gone in and had wandered up and down in the room for a while with the letter of the governor's wife in blue postal paper in his hand. He looked very much offended at Ma, when she seemed to think more about the load from the city than about his letter. She only suggested gently that they must talk about all that in the evening.

"All that—you say, Ma!—that Inger-Johanna is invited down there next winter—and we have Rönnow to thank for it. That is short and clear enough, I should think! What? What?" he roared out impatiently. "Is it not plain?—or have you some notions about it?"

"No—no, dear Jäger!"

"Well, then you should not delay the whole unloading of the goods with your quiet sigh, full of importance, and your secret meanings which always make me mad. You know I hate it! I go straight to the point always!"

"I was merely thinking about your uniform coat, whether the tailor has sent the pieces with it, you know—"

"You are right, you are right, Gitta," and out he rushed like a flash.

The unpacking went on in the kitchen, before the spice closet with its numerous compartments, where raisins, prunes, almonds, the different kinds of sugar, allspice, and cinnamon, were each put into their own places. Now and then fell a tribute, a prune, two almonds, three raisins, to each of the children; and it could not be denied that this load

CHAPTER II

from the city was like a foretaste of Christmas Eve.

At first the captain was intensely interested in getting hold of the ink bottles, the tobacco, and the strong wares which were to be kept in the cellar— everything else must be put aside for them. And then he flew in and out, with one bill or another in his hand and a quill pen full of ink, to compare with the general bill which his wife had nailed up on the upper door of the spice closet.

"Ma, can you conceive such extortion?" stopping suddenly before the bill, which still finally was always found to be right, and then turning thoughtfully round again, while he dried his pen in his chocolate-colored every-day wig.

His plethoric, vociferous, somewhat confused nature always became furious when he saw a bill; it operated like a red cloth on a bull, and when, as now, all the half year's bills came storming down on him at once, he both roared and bellowed. It was an old story for his wife, who had acquired a remarkable skill in taking the bull by the horns.

The wrongs, which thus he did *not* suffer, seemed nevertheless to awaken an increasing storm of resentment in him. With a violent tug at the door-latch, and his wig awry, he would come suddenly in, exclaiming,—"Seventy-five dollars, three shillings, seventeen pence!—seventy-five—dollars— three shillings—and seventeen pence!—it is almost enough to make one crazy. And so you ordered citron — citron,"— he put on a falsetto tone, and laughed out of pure rage. "He, he, he, he! — now have we the means for that? And then, almond soap for the guest-chamber!" This last came in a deep, suppressed, gloomy bass. "I cannot understand how you could have hit on that!"

"My dear, that was thrown in. Don't you see that it is n't carried out for anything?"

"Thrown in — oh, thrown in — yes, there you see how they cheat! Seventy-five dollars, three shillings, and seventeen pence — plainly that is enough to be frightened at. Where shall I find the money?"

"But you have already found it, Jäger! — Remember the servants," she whispered quickly. It was a quiet prayer to put off the rest of the outburst till later in the afternoon, between themselves.

The captain's various ecstatic flashes of passion about the bills went over the house that afternoon like a refreshing and purifying thunderstorm before Christmas. The children, cowed and tortured, took refuge during the storm under the protection of their mother, who warded off the blast; but when his step was again heard in the office, they went on, just as persevering and inquisitive as before, peeping into and shaking out the bags in order to find a raisin or two or a currant that had been forgotten, collecting the twine, looking after the weight, and cutting up the bar soap.

During all these anxieties the tall form of the

mistress stood in uninterrupted activity, bowed like a crane over the box with the city wares, which had been lifted in on the kitchen floor. Jars, willow baskets filled with hay, small bags, and an infinity of packages in gray wrappers, tied up with twine, small and great, vanished by degrees into their different resting-places, even to the last, the bag with the fine wheat flour, which was brought in by Great-Ola and put by itself in the meal-chest in the pantry.

When the spice closet was finally shut, the captain stood there for the twentieth time. With the air of a man who had been made to wait and been tormented long enough, he gently tapped her on the shoulder with his fingers and said, rather reproachfully, "It really astonishes me, Gitta, that you don't pay more attention to the letter we have received to-day."

"I have n't been able to think of anything else than your troubles with the bills, Jäger. Now I think you might taste the French brandy this evening, to see if it is good enough for the Christmas punch. Cognac is so dear."

"'That's a good idea, Gitta!—Yes, yes—only let us have supper soon."

The plates with oatmeal porridge and the blue milk in the cold cups were placed upon the table; they stood like black, dreary islands over the cloth, and presented no temptation to linger over the evening meal.

After the necessary part of it was swallowed and the children were sent upstairs, the captain sat, now quite cozy and comfortable, before the table, which was still extended, with his tobacco and his taste of toddy made of the French brandy, whose transformation into Christmas punch was going on in the kitchen, from which there was also heard the sizzling of the waffle-iron.

"Only strong, Ma,—only strong!—Then you can manage with the brown sugar.—Yes, yes," tasting of the wooden dipper which his wife brought in, "you can treat the sheriff to that with pleasure."

"Now Marit is coming in with the warm waffles, —and then it was this about the letter of the governor's wife.—You see, Jäger, we cannot send the child there unless we have her suitably fitted out; she must have a black silk confirmation dress, city boots and shoes, a hat, and other things."

"Black silk conf—"

"Yes, and some other dresses, which we must order in Christiania; there is no help for it."

Captain Jäger began to walk to and fro.

"So, so!—So, so! Well, if that is your idea, then I think we will decline the invitation with thanks."

"I knew that, Jäger! You would like to have the yolk, but as to breaking the egg, you hesitate."

"Break the egg? Break my purse, you mean."

"I mean, you can call in a part of the six hundred dollars you got with me. I have thought and

CHAPTER II

reckoned it over. Inger-Johanna alone will cost us over one hundred dollars this year, and when Thinka is going to Ryfylke, we shall not get off with two hundred."

"Over two hundred dollars!—Are you crazy? Are you crazy—really crazy, Ma? I think you have a screw loose!" He made a sudden turn over the floor. "The letter shall rather go at once into the stove."

"Very well; you know that I think everything you do is sensible, Jäger."

He stopped, with the letter in his hand and his mouth half open.

"And the slight chance Inger-Johanna might have of being provided for, that perhaps is not so much to be taken into account. She is certainly the nearest relation. There is nothing in the way to prevent her being the heir also.—N–no, do as you will and as you like, Jäger. You probably see more clearly in this than I do.—And then you will take the responsibility yourself, Jäger,"—she sighed.

The captain crumpled the letter together, gave her a hasty glance like a wounded lion, and then stood awhile and stared at the floor. Suddenly he threw the letter on the table and broke out: "She must go!—But the cost of the campaign—the cost of the campaign, Ma, that, I learned in my strategy, must be borne by the enemy! And the governor's wife must naturally take care of her outfit there."

"The governor's wife, Jäger, must not pay for anything—not a bit—before she has decided if she will keep her. We must not be anxious to be rid of her; but *she* shall be anxious to get her; and she must ask us for her, both once and twice, you understand."

That the winter was coming on was less noticed this year than usual. Two children were to be fitted out. Soon spinning-wheel and reel accompanied, in the short day and long evening, the murmur of the stove. Ma herself spun all the fine woof for the linsey-woolsey dresses. There was knitting, weaving, and sewing, nay, also embroidery on linen—"twelve of everything for each one." And in school hours in the office the captain worked not less zealously with the French grammar.

The stiffening cold frost, which blew about the house and cut like ice from every crack; the cold so fierce that the skin was torn off the hands when any one was unlucky enough to take hold of the latch of the outer door or of the porch without mittens; complaints of nail ache, when the children came in from out-of-doors; or else that the drinking-water was frozen solid in the tubs and pails, that the meat must be thawed out,—this was only what was usual in the mountain region. The doleful, monotonous howling and the long, hungry yelling of the wolves down on the ice could be heard from the

CHAPTER II

Gilje hills both by day and by night. The road on the lake lasted a long time. It was there till long into the spring thaw, though worn, unsafe, and blue with its dirt-brown mudstreak.

But when it did disappear, and the ice was melted by the heat of the sun, there lay on the steep hill behind the house a long line of bleaching linen, so shining white that it seemed as if the snow had forgotten to go away there.

Chapter III

IT was midsummer. The mountain region was hazy in the heat; all the distance was as if enveloped in smoke. The girls on the farm went about barefooted, in waists and short petticoats. It was a scorching heat, so that the pitch ran in sticky white lines down from the fat knots in the timber of the newly built pigsty, where Marit was giving swill to the hogs. Some sand-scoured wooden milk-pans stood on edge by the well, drying, while one or two sparrows and wagtails hopped about or perched nodding on the well-curb, and the blows of the axe resounded from the wood-shed in the quiet of the afternoon. Pasop lay panting in the shade behind the outer door, which stood open.

The captain had finished his afternoon nap, and stood by the field looking at Great-Ola and the horses ploughing up an old grassland which was to be laid down again.

The bumble-bee was humming in the garden. With about the same monotonous voice, Thinka and Inger-Johanna, sitting by the stone table in the summer-house over the cracked blue book-cover and the dog-eared, well-thumbed leaves, mumbled the Catechism and Commentary, with elbows and heads close to each other. They had to learn pages eighty-four to eighty-seven before supper time, and

CHAPTER III

they held their fingers in their ears so as not to disturb each other.

There was darkness like a shadow just outside of the garden fence. But they saw nothing, heard nothing; the long passage of Scripture went way over on the second page.

Then there was a gay clearing of a throat. "Might one interrupt the two young ladies with earthly affairs?"

They both looked up at the same time. The light hop leaves about the summer-house had not yet entirely covered the trellis.

With his arms leaning on the garden fence there stood a young man—he might have been standing there a long time—with a cap almost without a visor over thick brown hair. His face was sunburned and swollen.

The eyes, which gazed on them, looked dreadfully wicked.

Neither of them saw more; for, by a common impulse at the phenomenon, they ran in utter panic out of the door, leaving the books spread open behind them, and up the steps in to Ma, who was in the kitchen buttering bread for lunch.

"There was a man standing—there was a man out by the garden fence. It was certainly not any one who goes around begging or anything like that."

"Hear what he has to say, Jörgen," said Ma,

quickly comprehending the situation; "this way, out the veranda door. Appear as if you came of your own accord."

Both the girls flew in to the windows of the best room in order to peep out under the curtains.

He was coming in by the steps to the outer door with Jörgen, who suddenly vanished from his sight into the kitchen.

Little Thea stood in the door of the sitting-room with a piece of bread and butter, clutching the latch, and, holding the door half shut and half open, stared at him; she was altogether out of it.

"Is your father at home?"

"Yes, but you must go by the kitchen path, do you hear? And wait till we have had lunch; he is not going up to the office before that." She took him for a man who was going to be put on the roll.

"But I am not going to the office, you see."

Ma herself came now; she had managed to get her cap on in her hurry, but it was all awry.

"A young man, I see, who has perhaps come a long distance to-day. Please walk in."

Her smile was kind, but her eye underneath it was as sharp as an officer's review; here were holes and darns with coarse thread for the nonce and rents in abundance, and it was not easy to free herself from the suspicion of some questionable rover, especially when he dropped straight in through the door with the remark: "I come like a tramp from the mountain wilds, madam. I must make many excuses."

Ma's searching look had in the mean time broken through the shell. The white streak on the upper part of the forehead, under the shade where the skin had not been reddened by the sunburn, and his whole manner determined her to scrutinize him prudently. "Please sit down, Jäger is coming soon." She incidentally passed by the sewing-table and shut it. "Won't you let me send you a glass of milk in the mean time?"

A girl came in with a great basin, shaped like a bowl, and vanished again.

He put it to his mouth, noted with his eye how much he had drunk, drank again, and took another view.

"It is delightful—is not at all like the mistress of the house, for she seemed like sour milk, and"—he suppressed a sigh—"dangerously dignified."

He drank again.

"Yes, now one really must stop; but since and whereas—"

He placed the basin quite empty on the plate.

" Best to attack him at once. Dead broke, will you on my honest face lend me four—no, that does not sound well, better out with it at once—five dollars, so that I can get to Christiania?"

The small eyes twinkled quickly. If only the captain had come then! Some one was walking about out there.

He gazed abstractedly; he repeated his speech to himself. It was always altered, and now he stood again at the ticklish point—the amount. He considered if perhaps he only needed to ask for four—three?

There was a growling out in the hall; the dog rushed out, barking loudly. It was plainly the captain.

The young man rose hurriedly, but sat down again like a spring ready to jump up out of a chair: he had been in too great haste.

"In the parlor—some sort of fellow who wants to talk with me?" It was out on the stairs that some one was speaking.

A moment or two later, and the captain appeared in the door.

"I must beg you to excuse me, Captain. I have unfortunately, unfortunately"—here he began to stammer; bad luck would have it that one of the two young girls whom he had seen in the summer-house, the dark one, came in after her father; and so it would not do—"come over the mountain," he continued. "You will understand that one cannot exactly appear in the best plight." The last came in a tone of forced ease.

CHAPTER III

The captain at that moment did not appear exactly agreeably surprised.

"My name is Arent Grip!"

"Arent Grip!" rejoined the captain, looking at him. "Grip! the same phiz and eyes! You can never be the son of Perpetuum—cadet at Lurleiken? He is a farmer, or proprietor I suppose he calls himself, somewhere among the fjords."

"He is my father, Captain."

"Does he still work as hard as ever at his mechanical ideas?" asked the captain. "I heard that he had carried the water for his mill straight through the roof of the cow-barn, so that the cows got a shower bath, when the pipes sprung a leak."

Inger-Johanna caught a movement of indignation, as if the stranger suddenly grasped after his cap. "Shame, shame, that those times did not give a man like my father a scientific education." He said this with a seriousness utterly oblivious of the captain.

"So, so. Well, my boy, you must be kind enough to take a little lunch with us, before you start off. Inger-Johanna, tell Ma that we want something to drink and bread and butter. You must be hungry coming down from the mountains. Sit down.—And what is now your—your occupation or profession in the world? if I might ask." The captain sauntered around the floor.

"Student; and, Captain," he gasped, in order to use quickly the moment while they were alone, "since I have been so free as to come in here thus without knowing you—"

"Student!" The captain stopped in the middle of the floor. "Yes, I would have risked my head on it, saw it at the first glance, but yet I was a little in doubt. Well, yes," clearing his throat, "nearly plucked, perhaps; eh, boy?" inquired he good-naturedly. "Your father also had trouble with his examinations."

"I have not the fractional part of my father's brains, but with what I have, they gave me this year *laudabilis praeceteris*."

"Son of my friend, Fin Arentzen Grip!" He uttered each one of the names with a certain tender recognition. "Your father was, all things considered, a man of good ability, not to say a little of a genius,—when he failed in his officer's examination, it was all due to his irregular notions. Well, so you are his son! Yes, he wrote many a composition for me—the pinch was always with the compositions, you see."

"And, Captain," began the young man again earnestly, now in a louder and more decided tone, "since I can thus, without further ceremony, confidently address you—"

"You can tell Ma," said the captain, when Inger-Johanna again came in with her taller, over-

CHAPTER III

grown sister, "that it is Student Arent Grip, son of my old delightful comrade at the Military School."

The result of this last message was that the contemplated plate with a glass and bread and butter was changed to a little lunch for him and the captain, spread out on a tray.

The old bread-basket of red lacquer was filled with slices of black, sour bread, the crusts of which were cracked off. More's the pity, Ma declared, it had been spoiled in the baking, and the gray, heavy crust was due to the fact that so much of the grain on the captain's farm last year was harvested before it was ripe.

The student showed the sincerity of his forbearance of these defects through an absolutely murderous appetite. The prudential lumps of salt, which studded the fresh mountain butter with pearly tears in a superfluous abundance, he had a knack of dodging boldly and incisively, which did not escape admiring eyes; only a single short stroke of his knife on the under side of the bread and butter, and the lumps of salt rained and pattered over the plate.

"You will surely have some dried beef? I guess you have not had much to eat to-day. Go and get some more, Thinka. A little dram with the cheese, what? You can believe that we tested many a good old cheese in the den at your father's, and when we had a spree, we sent for it, and it circulated round from one party to another; and then the apples from Bergen which he got by the bushel by freighting-vessel from home! He was such a greenhorn, and so kind hearted—too confiding for such rascals as we! Oh, how we hunted through his closet and boxes!—and then we did our exercises at the same time; it was only his that the teacher corrected through the whole class." The captain emptied the second part of his long dram. "Ah!" He held his glass up against the light, and looked through it, as he was accustomed to. "But nevertheless, there was something odd about him, you know; you must see that such a one, straight from the country, does not fit in at once. Never forget when he first lectured us about perpetual motion. It was done with only five apples in a wheel, he said, and the apples must be absolutely mathematically exact. It was that which got out and ruined him, so people came to—yes, you know—comment on it, and make fun of him; and that hung on till the examination."

The student wriggled about.

The young ladies, who were sitting with their sewing by the window, also noticed how he had now forgotten himself; during the whole time he had kept one boot under the chair behind the other in order to conceal the sole of his shoes gaping wide open. They were in good spirits, and hardly dared to look at each other—son of a man who was called

CHAPTER III

Perpetuum, was a cadet, and gave the cows a bath. Father was dreadfully amusing when there were strangers present.

"Not a moment's doubt that there were ideas —but there was something obstinate about him. To come, as he did, straight from the farm, and then to begin to dispute with the teacher about what is in the book, never succeeds well, especially in physics in the Military School. And you can believe that was a comedy."

"Then I will bet my head that it was not my father who was wrong, Captain."

"Hm, hm—naturally yes, his father to a dot," he mumbled—"Hm, well, you have got *praeceteris* all the same,—will you have a drop more?" came the hospitable diversion.

"No, I thank you. But I will tell you how it was with my father. It was just as it was with a hound they had once at the judge's. There was such blood and spirit in him that you would search long to find his equal; but one day he bit a sheep, and so he had to be cured. It was done by locking him up in a sheepfold. There he stood, alone before the ram and all the sheepfold. It seemed to him splendid fun. Then the ram came leaping at him, and the dog rolled heels over head. Pshaw, that was nothing; but after the ram came tripping—before he could rise—all the fifty sheep trip—trip—trip, over him; then he was entirely confused. Again they stood opposite each other, and once more the ram rushed in on the dog, and trip — trip — trip — trip, came the feet of the whole flock of sheep over him. So they kept on for fully two hours, until the dog lay perfectly quiet and completely stunned. He was cured, never bit a sheep again. But what he was good for afterwards we had better not talk about — he had been through the Military School, Captain."

When he looked up, he met the dark, intense eyes of the mistress fixed on him; her capped head immediately bent down over the sewing again.

The captain had listened more and more eagerly. The cure of the hound interested him. It was only at the last expression he discovered that there was any hidden meaning in it.

"Hm — my dear Grip. Ah! Yes, you think that. Hm, can't agree with you. There were skilful teachers, and — ho, ho, — really we were not sheep — rather wolves to meet with, my boy. But the cure, I must admit, was disgraceful for a good dog, and in so far — well, a drop more?"

"Thank you, Captain."

"But what kind of a road do you say you have been over, my boy?"

With the food and the glass and a half of cordial which he had enjoyed, new life had come into the young man. He looked at his clothes, and was even so bold as to put his boots out; a great seam went across one knee.

CHAPTER III

"I certainly might be set up as a scarecrow for a terror and warning to all those who will depart from the highway. It was all because at the post station I met a deer-hunter, an excellent fellow. The chap talked to me so long of what there was on the mountain that I wanted to go with him."

"Extremely reasonable," muttered the captain, "when a man is paying for his son in Christiania."

"I had become curious, I must tell you, and so started off for the heart of the mountains."

"Is he not even more aggravatingly mad than his father,—to start in haphazard over the black, pathless mountain?"

"The track led over the débris and stones at the foot at first for five hours. But I don't know what it is upon the mountain; it was as if something got into my legs. The air was so fine and light, as if I had been drinking champagne; it intoxicated me. I should have liked to walk on my hands, and it would have been of no consequence to any one in the whole wide world, for I was on the summit. And never in my life have I seen such a view as when we stood, in the afternoon, on the mountain crest,—only cool, white, shining snow, and dark blue sky, peak on peak, one behind the other, in a glory as far as the eye could reach."

"Yes, we have snow enough, my boy. It stands close up against the walls of the house here all winter, as clear, white, and cold as any one could wish.

We find ourselves very well satisfied with that,—but show me a beautiful green meadow or a fine field of grain, my boy."

"It seemed to me as if one great fellow of a mountain stood by the side of another and said: You poor, thin-legged, puny being, are you not going to be blown away in the blue draught, here on the snow-field, like a scrap of paper? If you wish to know what is great, take your standard from us."

"You got *praeceteris*, you said, my man? Yes, yes, yes, yes! What do you say if we get the shoemaker to put a little patch on your shoes to-night?"

It was as much as an invitation to stay all night!—Extremely tempting to postpone the request till next day. "Thank you, Captain, I will not deny that it might be decidedly practical."

"Tell the shoemaker, Jörgen, to take them as soon as he has put the heel-irons on those I am to have for the survey of the roads."

Oh! So he is going away, perhaps early to-morrow morning; it must be done this evening, nevertheless! Now, when the daughters were beginning to clear off the table, it was best to watch his chance.

The captain began walking up and down the floor with short steps. "Yes, yes, true! Yes, yes, true! Would you like to see some fine pigs, Grip?"

CHAPTER III

The student immediately sprang up. The way out! He grabbed his cap. "Do you keep many, Captain?" he asked, extremely interested.

"Come!—oh, it is no matter about going through the kitchen—come out a little while on the porch steps. Do you see that light spot in the woods up there? That is where we took the timber for the cow-house and the pigsty, two years ago."

He went out into the farmyard bare-headed.

"Marit, Marit, here is some one who wants to see your pigs. Now you shall be reviewed. There are a sow and seven—you see. Ugh, ugh, yes. Hear your little ones, Marit!—But it was the brick wall, you see. Right here was a swamp hole; it oozed through from the brook above. And now—see the drain there?—as dry as tinder."

Now or never the petition must be presented.

"And now they live like lords all together there," continued the captain.

"All seven of the dollars—what am I saying, all five of the pigs."

"What?"

"Here is your hat, father!"—Jörgen came from the house—"and there are some of the people down from Fosse standing there and waiting."

"So? We will only just look into the stable a little."

There stood Svarten and Brunen, just unharnessed, still dripping wet and with stiff hair after the work at the plough.

"Fine stall, eh?—and very light; the horses don't come out of the door half blind. Ho, Svarten, are you sweaty now?"

There was a warm and pleasant smell of the stable—and finally—

"Captain, I am going to make a re—"

"But, Ola," interrupted the latter, "see Brunen's crib there! I don't like those bits. It can't be that he bites it?"

"Ha, ha, ha—no, by no means." Ola grinned slyly; he was not going to admit in a stranger's presence that the captain's new bay was a cribber!

The captain had become very red; he pulled off his cap, and hurriedly walked along with it in his hand—"such a rascal of a horse-trader!"

He no longer looked as if he would listen to a request.

Out of the afternoon shade by the stable walls the two men just spoken of appeared.

"Is this a time of day to come to people?" he blurted out. "Ah well—go up to the office."

At this he strode over the yard, peeped into the well, and turned towards the window of the sitting-room.

"Girls! Inger-Johanna—Thinka," he called in a loud tone. "Ask Ma if that piece of meat is going to lie there by the well and rot."

CHAPTER III

"Marit has taken it up, we are going to have it for supper," Thinka tried to whisper.

"Oh! Is it necessary on that account to keep it where Pasop can get it?—Show the student down into the garden, so that he can get some currants," he called out of the door, as he went up by the stables to his office.

Arent Grip's head, covered with thick brown hair, with the scanty flat cap upon it, could now be seen for a good long time among the currant bushes by the side of Thinka's little tall, blond one. At first he talked a great deal, and the sprightly, bright, brown eyes were not in the least wicked, Thinka thought. She began to feel rather a warm interest in him.

He found his boots in the morning standing mended before his bed, and a tray with coffee and breakfast came up to him. He had said he must be off early.

Now it all depended on making his decisive leap with closed eyes in the dark.

When he came down, the captain stood on the stairs with his pipe. Over his fat neck, where the buckle of his military stock shone, grayish locks of hair stuck out under his reddish wig. He was looking out a little discontentedly into the morning fog, speculating on whether it would settle or rise so that he would dare order the mowing to go on.

"So you are going to start, my boy?"

"Captain, can — will you lend me — " in his first courage of the morning he had thought of five, but it sank to four even while he was on the stairs, and now in the presence of the captain to — "three dollars? I have used up every shilling I had to get to Christiania with. You shall have them by money order immediately."

The captain hemmed and hawed. He had almost suspected something of the sort yesterday in the fellow's face — yes, such a student was the kind of a fellow to send back a money order!

There began to be a sort of an ugly grin on his face. But suddenly he assumed a good-natured, free and easy mien. "Three dollars, you say? — If I had three in the house, my boy! But here, by fits and starts in the summer, it is as if the ready money was clean swept away." He stuck his unoccupied hand in the breast of his uniform coat, and looked vacantly out into the air. "Ah! hm-hm," came after a dreadfully oppressive pause. "If I was only sure of getting them back again, I would see if I could pick up three or four shillings at any rate in Ma's household box — so that you could get down to the sheriff or the judge. They are excellent people, I know them; they help at the first word."

The captain, puffing vigorously at his pipe, went into the kitchen to Ma, who was standing in the

CHAPTER III

pantry and dealing out the breakfast. She had the hay-making and the whole of the outside affairs upon her shoulders.

He was away quite a little time.

"Well, if Ma did not have the three dollars after all! So I have got them for you. And so good-by from Gilje! Let us hear when you get there."

"You shall hear in a money order," and the student strode jubilantly away.

It is true that at first Ma had stopped for a moment and pinched her lips together, and then she had declared as her most settled opinion that, if the captain was going to help at all, it must be with all three. He did not seem one of those who shirked everything—was not one who was all surface—and it would not do at all to let him beg at the judge's, the sheriff's, and perhaps the minister's, because he could not get a loan of more than three shillings at Gilje.

From time to time Thinka told of all that she and the student had talked about together.

"What did he say then?" urged Inger-Johanna.

"Oh, he was entertaining almost all the time; I have never heard any one so entertaining."

"Yes, but do you remember that he said anything?"

"Oh, yes, he asked why you were reading

French. Perhaps you were to be trained to be a parrot, so that you could chatter when you came to the city."

"So,— how did he know that I was going to the city?"

"He asked how old you were; and then I said that you were to be confirmed and to go there. He was very well acquainted at the governor's house; he had done extra writing, or something of that sort, at the office, since he had been a student."

"That kind of acquaintance, yes."

"But you would n't suit exactly there, he said; and do you know why?"

"No."

"Do you want to know? He thought you had too much backbone."

"What—did he say?"

She wrinkled her eyebrows and looked up sharply, so that Thinka hastened to add: "Whoever comes there must be able to wind like a sewing thread around the governor's wife, he said; it would be a shame for your beautiful neck to get a twist so early."

Inger-Johanna threw her head back and smiled: "Did you ever hear such a man!"

. . . .

Thinka had gone to Ryfylke. Her place at the table, in the living-room, in the bed-chamber, was empty air. The captain started out time after time to call her.

And now the last afternoon had come, when Inger-Johanna was also going away.

The sealskin trunk with new iron bands stood open in the hall ready for packing. The cariole was standing in the shed, greased so that the oil was running out of the ends of the axles, and Great-Ola, who was to start the next morning on the three days' journey, was giving Svarten oats.

The captain had been terribly busy that day: no one understood how to pack as he did.

Ma handed over to him one piece of the new precious stuff after the other; the linen from Gilje would bear the eye of the governor's wife.

But the misfortune of it was that the blood rushed so to Jäger's head when he stooped over.

"Hullo, good! I don't understand what you are thinking of, Ma, to come with all that load of cotton stockings at once! It is this, this, this I want."

Naturally, used to travelling as he was—"But it is so bad for you to stoop over, Jäger."

He straightened up hurriedly. "Do you think Great-Ola has the wit to rub Svarten with Riga liniment on the bruise on his neck and to take the bottle with him in his bag? If I had not thought of that now, Svarten would have had to trot with it. Run down and tell him that, Thea.—Oh, no!"

he drew a despairing breath; "I must go myself, and see that it is done right."

There was a pause until his footfall had ceased to creak on the lowest step. Then Ma began to pack with precipitous haste: "It is best to spare your father from the rush of blood to his head."

The contents of the trunk rose layer upon layer, until the white napkin was at last spread over it and covered the whole, and it only remained to sit upon the lid and force the key to turn in the lock.

Towards supper time the worst hubbub and trouble were over. Ma's hasty-pudding, as smooth as velvet, with raspberry sauce, was standing on the table, and solemnly reminded them that again there would be one less in the daily circle.

They ate in silence without any other sound than the rattling of the spoons.

"There, child, take my large cup. Take it when your father bids you."

Certainly she is beautiful, the apple of his eye. Only look at her hands when she is eating! She is as delicate and pale as a nun.

He sighed, greatly down-hearted, and shoved his plate from him.

Tears burst from Inger-Johanna's eyes.

No one would have any more.

Now he walked and whistled and gazed on the floor.

It was a pity to see how unhappy father was.

CHAPTER III

"You must write every month, child—at length and about everything—do you hear?—large and small, whatever you are thinking of, so that your father may have something to take pleasure in," Ma admonished, while they were clearing off the table. "And listen now, Inger-Johanna," she continued when they were alone in the pantry: "If it is so that the governor's wife wants to read your letters, then put a little cross by the signature. But if there is anything the matter, tell it to old Aunt Alette out in the bishop's mansion; then I shall know it when Great-Ola is in for the city load. You know your father can bear so little that is disagreeable."

"The governor's wife read what I write to you and father! That I will defy her to do."

"You must accommodate yourself to her wishes, child. You can do it easily when you try, and your aunt is extremely kind and good to those she likes, when she has things her own way. You know how much may depend on her liking you, and—you understand—getting a little fond of you. She has certainly not asked you there without thinking of keeping you in the place of a daughter."

"Any one else's daughter? Take me from you and father? No, in that case I would rather never go there."

She seated herself on the edge of the meal-chest and began to sob violently.

"Come, come, Inger-Johanna." Ma stroked her hair with her hand. "We do not wish to lose you; you know that well enough,"—her voice trembled. "It is for your own advantage, child. What do you think you three girls have to depend upon, if your father should be taken away? We must be glad if a place offers, and even take good care not to lose it; remember that, always remember that, Inger-Johanna. You have intelligence enough, if you can also learn to control your will; that is your danger, child."

Inger-Johanna looked up at her mother with an expression almost of terror. She had a bitter struggle to understand. In her, in whom she had always found aid, there was suddenly a glimpse of the helpless.

"I can hardly bear to lose the young one out of my sight to-night, and you leave me alone in there," came the captain, creaking in the door. "You haven't a thought of how desolate and lonesome it will be for me, Ma." He blew out like a whale.

"We are all coming in now, and perhaps father will sing a little this evening," Ma said encouragingly.

The captain's fine, now a little hoarse, bass was his pride and renown from his youth up.

The clavichord was cleared of its books and papers

—the cover must be entirely lifted when father was to sing.

It stood there with its yellow teeth, its thin, high tone, and its four dead keys; and Ma must play the accompaniment, in which always, in some part or other, she was left lying behind, like a sack that has fallen out of a wagon, while the horse patiently trots on over the road. His impatience she bore with stoical tranquillity.

This evening he went through *Heimkringlas panna, du höga Nord,* and *Vikingebalken,* to

> *Lo! the chase's empress cometh! Hapless Frithjof, glance away!*
> *Like a star on spring cloud sitteth she upon her courser gray.*

He sang so that the window-panes rattled.

Chapter IV

THE year had turned. It was as long after Christmas as the middle of February.

In the evening the captain was sitting, with two candles in tin candlesticks, smoking and reading *Hermoder*. At the other end of the table the light was used by Jörgen, who was studying his lessons; he must worry out the hours that had been assigned, whether he knew the lessons or not.

The frosty panes shone almost as white as marble in the moonlight, which printed the whole of a pale window on the door panel in the lower, unlighted end of the sitting-room.

Certainly there were bells!

Jörgen raised his head, covered with coarse, yellow hair, from his book. It was the second time he had heard them, far away on the hill; but, like the sentinels of Haakon Adelstensfostre at the beacon, of whom he was just reading, he did not dare to jump up from his reading and give the alarm until he was sure.

"I think there are bells on the road," he gently remarked, "far off."

"Nonsense! attend to your lesson."

But, notwithstanding he pretended that he was deeply absorbed in the esthetic depths of *Hermoder*, the captain also sat with open ears.

"The trader's bells—they are so dull and low," Jörgen put in again.

"If you disturb me again, Jörgen, you shall hear the bells about your own ears."

The trader, Öjseth, was the last one the captain could think of wishing to see at the farm. He kept writing and writing after those paltry thirty dollars of his, as if he believed he would lose them. "Hm! hm!" He grew somewhat red in the face, and read on, determined not to see the man before he was standing in the room.

The bells plainly stopped before the door.

"Hm! hm!"

Jörgen moved uneasily.

"If you move off the spot, boy, I'll break your arms and legs in pieces!" foamed the captain, now red as copper. "Sit—sit still and read!"

He intended also to sit still himself. That scoundrel of a trader—he should fasten his horse himself at the doorsteps, and help himself as he could.

"I hear them talking—Great-Ola."

"Hold your tongue!" said the captain in a murderous deep bass, and with a pair of eyes fixed on his son as if he could eat him.

"Yes; but, father, it is really—"

A pull on his forelock and a box on the ears sent him across the floor.

"The doctor," roared Jörgen.

The truth of his martyrdom was established in the same moment, because the short, square form of the military doctor appeared in the door.

His fur coat was all unbuttoned, and the tip of his long scarf trailed behind him on the threshold. He held his watch out: "What time is it?"

"Now, then, may the devil take your body and soul to hell, where you long ago belonged, if it isn't you, Rist!"

"What time is it? I say — Look!"

"And here I go and lick Jörgen for — well, well, boy, you shall be excused from your lesson and can ask for syrup on your porridge this evening. Go out to Ma, and tell her Rist is here."

The captain opened the kitchen door: "Hullo, Marit! Siri! A girl in here to pull off the doctor's boots! All the diseases of the country are in your clothes."

"What time is it, I say — can you see?"

"Twenty-five minutes of seven."

"Twenty-one miles in two hours and a quarter — from Jölstad here, with my bay!"

The doctor had got his fur coat off. The short, muscular man, with broad face and reddish-gray whiskers, stood there in a fur cap, swallowed up in a pair of long travelling boots.

"No, no," he exclaimed to the girl, who was making an effort to pull them off. "Oh, listen, Jäger;

will you go out and feel of the bay's hind leg, if there is a wind-gall? He began to stumble a little, just here on the hill, I thought, and to limp."

"He has very likely got bruised." The captain eagerly grabbed his hat from the clavichord and went with him.

Outside by the sleigh they stood, thinly clothed in the severe frost, and felt over the hamstring and lifted up the left hind foot of the bay. For a final examination, they went into the stable.

When they came out there was a veritable wild dispute.

"I tell you, you might just as well have said he had glanders in his hind legs. If you are not a better judge of curing men than you are of horses, I would n't give four shillings for your whole medical examination."

"That brown horse of yours, Jäger — that is a strange fodder he takes. Does n't he content himself with crib-splinters?" retorted the doctor, slyly bantering.

"What? Did you see that, you — knacker?"

"Heard it, heard it; he gnawed like a saw there in the crib. He has cheated you unmercifully — that man from Filtvedt, you know."

"Oh, oh, in a year he will be tall enough for a cavalry horse. But this I shall concede, it was a good trade when you got the bay for sixty-five."

"Sixty and a binding dram, not a doit more. But I would not sell him, if you offered me a hundred on the spot."

Ma was waiting in her parlor.

Now, it was Aslak of Vaelta who had cut his foot last Thursday hewing timber—Ma had bandaged him—and then Anders, who lived in the cottage, was in a lung fever. The parish clerk had been there and bled him; six children up in that hut—not good if he should be taken away.

"We will put a good Spanish-fly blister on his back, and, if that does not make him better, then a good bleeding in addition."

"He came near fainting the last time," suggested Ma, doubtfully.

"Bleed—bleed—it is the blood which must be got away from the chest, or the inflammation will make an end of him. I will go and see him to-morrow morning—and for Thea's throat, camphor oil and a piece of woollen cloth, and to bed to sweat—and a good spoonful of castor-oil to-night—you can also rub the old beggar woman about the body with camphor, if she complains too much. I will give you some more."

After supper the old friend of the house sat with his pipe and his glass of punch at one end of the sofa, and the captain at the other. The red tint of the doctor's nose and cheeks was not exclusively to be attributed to the passage from the cold to the

CHAPTER IV

snug warmth of the room. He had the reputation of rather frequently consoling his bachelorhood with ardent spirits.

They had talked themselves tired about horses and last year's reminiscences of the camp, and had now come to more domestic affairs.

"The news, you see, is blown here both from the city and the West; old Aunt Alette wrote before Christmas that the governor's wife had found out she must drive with both snaffle and curb."

"I thought so," said the doctor, chewing his mouthpiece. "The first thing of importance in managing is to study the nature of the beast; and Inger-Johanna's is to rear; she must be treated gently."

"And that sister-in-law never believed that so much inborn stuff could grow up in the wild mountain region."

The captain began to puff impatiently. Ma would surely sometime get supper ready and come in, so he could get to his daughter's letters.

"You can believe he is a real pelican, that old judge down in Ryfylke! Orders them round and bellows—keeps them hot both in the office and in the house. I wonder if he won't sometime apply for an office somewhere else; for that is what he threatens to do every time he sees an office vacant, Thinka writes. Let us have the letters, Ma, and my spectacles," he exclaimed, when she came in. "The first is of November, so you shall hear about your goddaughter's coming to the governor's, Rist."

He hummed over a part of the beginning and then read:

When Great-Ola put my baggage inside the street door, I almost wanted to seat myself in the cariole and drive the three days home again; but then at once I thought, best to march straight on, as father says! I went past the servant and inside the hall door. It was very light there, and a great many outside garments and hats and caps were hanging on the pegs, and twice two servant-girls flew through with trays and teacups, without troubling themselves about me in the least. But I thought that the one who had fallen into the midst of things was your beloved daughter. My outside garments were off in a jiffy; I knocked once, twice, three times. I hardly knew what to do with myself, so I gently turned the knob. Thank heaven, there was no one there. There was another door with a portière, which I only needed to shove a little aside, and then—I was plunged right into the centre of it. Nay, how shall I describe it? It was a corner room that I had entered: there was only mahogany furniture and upholstered easy chairs, and pictures in gilded frames over the sofa; the other pictures were in dark frames; but I did not see a doit of all that, for I thought at first that it was dark. But it was n't dark at all. There was just a shade over the astral lamp on the table, and neither more nor less than a whole company. There in the lion's den, with the married ladies on the corner sofa, sat a number of people drinking tea.

I stood there in the middle of the floor, and the reddish brown linsey-woolsey, I believed, could surely defend itself.

"Aunt Zittow," I ventured.

"Who is it?—What? Can it be my dear Inger-Johanna? My husband's niece!" was said from the table. "You have come just like a wild mountain rose, child, with the rain still on your face—and so cold!" as she touched me. But I saw very well that she had her eye on my dress. I am sure it is too long in the waist, I thought; that is what I said at home. But then I forgot the whole dress, for it was indeed my aunt, and she embraced me and said, "You are heartily welcome, my dear child! I think now a cup of good hot tea will do her good, Miss Jörgensen,—and will you ask Mina to put her room in order upstairs!" And then she seated me on a soft cushioned chair by the side of the wall.

There I sat in the twilight, with a teacup in my lap, and biscuits—how I got them I cannot remember—and thought, is it I or not I?

At first it was not easy to see those who sat about in the soft stuffed chairs; what I saw nearest to me was a piece of a foot, with spurs and a broad red stripe along the side, which rocked up and down the whole time. Now and then a head with a fine lace cap bobbed up into the light to put down a cup or to replenish it. The lamp-shade made just a round ring in the room, not a foot from the table.

Oh, how warm and delicate it was!

In the light under the astral lamp-shade, aunt was sitting, bowed down over a little black contrivance with the image of a negro on it, and was burning pastilles; her hair, on both sides of her forehead, was made into stiff, grayish curls.

The bright, shining tea-kettle stood singing over the beautiful blue cups of that old Copenhagen porcelain, of which you have four pairs in the cabinet, which came from grandmother's. I could not help looking all the time on aunt's face, with the great earrings showing through the lace. I thought the antique tea-kettle, which is like a vase or urn, resembled her so much, with the haughty stiff curve of her chin! It was just as if they belonged together from—I don't know from what time, it could not be from the time of the creation, I suppose. And then when the conversation among them came to a stop and it was still as if there were not a human being there, the machine puffed and snorted as it were with aunt's fine Danish twist to the R: *Arvet! Arvet!* (inherited)—and in between it bubbled Zittow, von Zittow. It was what you told me, mother, about the Danish Zittow, who was diplomatist in Brussels, that was buzzing in me.

"The young one! She has got it in her blood," whinnied the doctor.

But it really did not look as if aunt thought there was any hurry about seeing uncle. And then when aunt sent Miss Jörgensen with some tea into the next room, where they were playing cards, I at once asked if I could be allowed to go with her.

"With all my heart, my child, it would be a shame to tax your patience any longer. And then, Miss Jörgensen, take our little traveller up to her room, and see that she has something to eat, and let her go to bed." But I saw very plainly that she pulled the lamp-shade down on the side I was going; that I thought of afterwards.

"What? what? what?" said my uncle. You should have seen him gaze at me. He looked so much like you, mother, about the forehead and eyes that I threw my arms around his neck.

He held me before him with his arms stretched out. "But really I think it is Aunt Eleonore all over! Well, well, now don't fancy you are such a beauty!"

That was the reception.

Shortly after I was lying in bed in my elegant

little blue room, with curtains with long fringes. There were pastilles on the stove, and Miss Jörgensen—just think, she called me Miss!—almost undressed me and put me between all the soft down quilts.

There I lay and thought it all over, and became hotter and hotter in my head and face, till at last it seemed as if I was thumping in the cariole with Svarten and Ola.

"No, the cariole came home again empty," said the captain with a sigh.

"Look out if you don't get her back to Gilje again in a carriage," added the doctor.

"She was so handsome, Rist," exclaimed the captain, quite moved. "It seems as if I see her, standing there in the middle of the floor at brother-in-law's, with her heavy black hair dressed up on her neck. From the time when she used to run about here, with the three long braids down her back, it was as if she developed into a swan all at once, when she came to dress in the clothes of a full-grown person—You remember her on confirmation day, Rist?"

"But, dear Jäger," said Ma, trying to subdue him.

The captain cautiously unfolded a letter, closely written on a large sheet of letter paper.

"And now you shall hear; this is dated January 23d."

CHAPTER IV

The money which I brought with me—

"Well, well—"

The bill of Larsen for—

"You can certainly skip over to the next page," remarked Ma with a certain emphasis.
"Well, yes, hm, hm,— mere trifles— here it is."

To think that father, and you also, mother, cannot see my two new dresses! Aunt is inconceivably good. It is impossible to walk any other way than beautifully in this kind of shoes; and that aunt says I do; it is just as if you always felt a dancing-floor under your feet. And yesterday aunt gave me a pair of patent leather sandals with buckles on the ankles. Did you ever hear of such! Yes— I kissed her for that, too, this time; she could say what she liked. For you must know, she says that the first rule of life for a lady is a kind of confident, reserved repose, which, however, may be cordial! I have it naturally, aunt says, and only need to cultivate it. I am going to learn to play on the piano and go through a regular course of lessons in dancing.

Aunt is so extremely good to me, only she will have the windows shut when I want them open. Of course I don't mean in the sitting-room, where they have pasted themselves in with double panes, but up in my own room. Just fancy, first double windows and then stuffy curtains, and then all the houses, which are near us across the street; you can't breathe, and much use it is to air out the rooms by the two upper panes twice a day!

Aunt says that I shall gradually get accustomed to the city air. But I don't see how I can, when I never get acquainted with it. Not once during the whole winter have I frozen my fingers! We go out for a short drive in the forenoon, and then I go with aunt in the shops in the afternoon, and that is the whole of it. And you can believe it is quite another thing to go out here than at home; when I only jumped over a little pile of shovelled-up snow, in order to get into the sleigh more quickly, aunt said that every one could instantly see manners from my state of nature, as she always says. For all the movements I make, I might just as well have chains on both legs, like the prisoners we see some days in the fort.

And now aunt wants me not to go bare-footed on the floor of my chamber. Nay, you should have seen her horror when I told her how Thinka and I, at the time of the breaking up of the ice last year, waded across the mill stream in order to avoid the roundabout way by the bridge! At last I got her to laughing with me. But I certainly believe that the pair of elegant slippers with swans-

CHAPTER IV

down on them, which stuck out of a package this morning, are for me! You see now, it is into them, nevertheless, that my sweet little will must be put.

"She is on her guard lest they should want to put a halter about her neck," mumbled the doctor.

Ma sighed deeply. "Such sweet small wills are so apt to grow into big ones, and"—again a sigh—"women don't get on in the world with that."

The doctor looked meditatively down into his glass: "One of woman's graces is flexibility, they say; but on the other hand, she is called 'proud maiden' in the ballad. There is something like a contradiction in that."

"Oh, the devil! Divide them into two platoons! It is mostly the ugly who have to be pliable," said the captain.

"Beauty does not last so very long, and so it is best to think of the years when one has to be accommodating," remarked Ma, down in her knitting-work.

The captain continued reading the letter.

The French is done in a twinkling. I am always ready with that before breakfast, and aunt is so contented with my pronunciation; but then the piano comes from nine to eleven. Ugh! only exercises; and then aunt receives calls. Guess who came day before yesterday? No one else than Student Grip. It was just as if I must have known him ever so well, and liked him even better, so glad was I at last to see any one who knew about us at home. But just think, I am not entirely sure that he did not try to dictate to aunt; and then he had the boldness to look at me as if I should agree with him. Aunt helped him to a place in uncle's office, because she heard that he had passed such an excellent examination and was so gifted, but had almost nothing from home to study on.

"I ventured my three dollars on him—But how the fellow could manage to take such high honors passes my comprehension," threw out the captain.

"But he repaid them all right, Jäger, with postage and everything."

The captain held the letter up to the light again.

And then aunt thought he would be the better for a little polish in his ways, and enjoined him to come to her fortnightly receptions; she likes to have young people about her; but he let aunt see that he regarded that as a command and compulsion. And now he came in fact to make a sort of excuse. But how they talked!

"Well, then, we shall see you again at some of our Thursday evenings?" said aunt.

"Your ladyship no doubt remembers the occasion of my remaining away. It was my ill-bred objections to the seven unanimous teacups which gave supreme judgment in your celebrated small tea-fights."

"See, see, see," aunt smiled. "I can't be wrong when I say that you are really made for social life; there is need just there for all one's best sides."

"All one's smoothest, your ladyship means."

"Well, well, no falling back, Mr. Grip, I beg you."

"I did my best, your ladyship; for I really thought all one's most mendacious."

"Now you are in the humor of contradiction again; and there one gets entangled so easily, you know."

"I only think that when one does not agree with what is said, and keeps silent, one lies."

"Then people offer up to good form, without which no social intercourse can exist."

"Yes, what do they offer up? Truth!"

"Perhaps more correctly a little of their vanity, an opportunity of exhibiting some bright and shining talent; that tempts young men greatly, I believe."

"Possible, not impossible at any rate," he admitted.

"Do you see?" But then aunt said, for she never abandons her text: "A little good manners is not out of place; and when I see a bright young student stand talking with his hands in his pockets, or riding backwards on a chair, then, whether the one concerned takes my motherly candor ill or not, I always try by a little hint to adjust the defects in his education."

You should have seen him! Hands out of his pockets, and at once he sat up before her, as straight as a candle.

"If all were like your ladyship, I would recommend making calls," said he, "for you are an honest woman."

"Woman! We say, lady."

"I mean an honest governor's lady; besides, I don't at all say a good-natured!" and then he shook that great brown lock of hair down over his forehead.

I do not need to wish for any portrait of you, for I lie thinking, in the evenings, that I am at home. I see father so plainly, walking up and down the room whistling, and then starting off up the office stairs; and I pull your hair, Jörgen! and poke your head down into the geography, so that I get you after me, and we run round, in one door and out another, up and down in the house. Nay, I long horribly at times. But I must not let aunt see that; it would be ungrateful. She does not believe that one can exist anywhere but in a city.

And then there are a lot of things which I have been obliged to draw a black mark through, because I don't at all understand them. Only think, mother! Aunt says, that it may at most be allowable to say that we have cows at home; but I must not presume to say that any one of them has a calf!" I should like to know how they think we get new cows, when we kill the old ones for Christmas?

Here the captain interpolated some inarticulate noises. But an expression of anxiety came over Ma's face, and she said faintly:

"That is because, unfortunately, we have not been able to keep the children sufficiently away from the servants' room, and from everything they hear there."

"You see, madam," declared the doctor, "in the city people are so proper that a hen hardly dares to lay eggs— It is only the products of the efforts of the land that they are willing to recognize, I can tell you."

"No," the captain put in, "it is not advisable for a poor mare to be so indiscreet as to have a foal there."

His wife coughed gently and made an errand to her sewing-table.

Ma had been gone upstairs for more than an hour, and the clock was getting on towards twelve.

The captain and the doctor were now sitting somewhat stupidly over the heeltaps in their mugs, a little like the dying tallow candles, which stood with neglected wicks, almost burned down into the sockets and running down.

"Keep your bay, Rist. Depend on me — he has got to get up early who takes me in on a horse — with my experience, you see. All the cavalry horses I have picked out in my time!"

The doctor sat looking down into his glass.

"You are thinking of the cribber," said the captain, getting into a passion; "but that was the most rascally villainy — pure cheating. He might have been taken into court for that — But, as I tell you, keep your bay."

"I have become a little tired of him, you see."

"See there, see there, — but that is your own fault and not the bay's, my boy. You are always tired of the beast you have. If you should count all the horses you have swapped, it would be a rare stable."

"They spoiled him for driving when he was a colt; he is one-sided, he is."

"That's all bosh. I should cure him of that in a fortnight, with a little breaking to harness."

"Oh, I am tired of sitting and pulling and hauling on one rein to keep him out of the side of the ditch; if it were not for that, the beast should never go out of my hand. No, had it been only that he made a few splinters in the crib."

The captain assumed a thoughtful expression; he leaned against the back of the sofa, and gave two or three deep, strong pulls on his pipe.

CHAPTER IV

"But my Brunen is nothing at all to talk about—a little gnawing only—with the one eye-tooth."

"Nay, my bay also gives way only on one side of the road."

Again two or three sounding puffs. The captain gave his wig a poke.

"If there is any one who could cure him of that, it is certainly I."

Dense smoke poured out of his pipe.

Over in his corner of the sofa the doctor began to clean his out.

"Besides, my Brunen is a remarkably kind animal—thunders a little on the crib down in the stall—a horse can hardly have less of a fault, and then so thoroughly easy on the rein—knows if one only touches it—so extremely sensitive in his mouth—a regular beauty to drive on the country road."

"Ye-s, ye-s; have nothing against that—fine animal!"

"Look here, Rist! All things considered, that was a driving horse for you—stands so obediently, if one just lays the rein over his back."

"Swap off the bay, do you mean?" pondered the doctor, in a doubting tone,—"had n't really thought of that." He shook his head—"Only I can't understand why he is so stiff on one rein."

"No, my boy; but I can understand it."

"If you are only not cheated in that, Jäger—trade is trade, you know."

"I cheated? Ha, ha, ha!" The captain shook with laughter and with quiet consciousness. "Done, boy! We will swap."

"You are rather quick on the rein, Jäger."

"Always my nature, you see—to get the thing closed up at once, on the nail. And so we will take a drink to close the bargain," shouted the captain eagerly; he pulled his wig awry, and sprang up.

"Let us see if Ma has some cognac in the closet."

What sort of a trick was it the horse had?

The captain was wholly absorbed in breaking the bay to harness. The horse turned his head to the right, and kept over on the side of the road just as far as he could for the rein. It was impossible to find any reason for it.

This morning he had broken off one of the trace-pins by driving against the gate-post. Was it possible that he was afraid of a shadow? That was an idea!—and the captain determined to try him in the moonlight that evening.

When he came down to the stable after dinner, he saw a wonderful sight.

Great-Ola had taken the bay out of his stall, and was standing shaking his fist against the horse's forehead.

"Well, I have tried him every way, Captain, but he wouldn't wink, not even if I broke his skull with the back of an axe—he doesn't move! And now see how he jumps!" He raised his hand towards the other side of the horse's head. "But in his left eye he is as blind as a shut cellar door."

The captain stood awhile without saying a word; the veins on his forehead swelled up blue, and his face became as red as the collar on his uniform coat.

"Well, then." In a rage he gave Ola a box on his ears. "Are you standing there threatening the horse, you dog?"

When Ola was feeding the horse at night, the captain went into the stall. He took the lantern and let it shine on the bay. "No use to cure you of going into the ditch—See there, Ola, take that shilling, so that you at all events may profit by it."

Ola's broad face lighted up with cunning. "The doctor must provide himself with planks, for the one he got ate up three two-inch boards while we had him."

"Look here, Ola," nodded the captain, "it is not worth while to let him hear anything but that the bay can see with both eyes here with us."

When Great-Ola, in breaking-up time in spring, was driving a load of wood home from the Gilje ridge, he was obliged to turn out on a snow-drift for Dr. Rist, who was coming in a sleigh from the north.

"Driving with the bay, I see. Has the captain

got him so that he's all right? Does he cling just as hard to the side of the road?"

"No, of course not. The captain was the man to make that all right. He is no more one-sided now than I am."

"As if I was going to believe that, you liar," mumbled the doctor, while he whipped his horse and drove on.

Chapter V

THE captain was in a dreadful humor; the doors were banging the whole forenoon.

At dinner time there was a sultry breathing spell, during which Jörgen and Thea sat with their eyes on their plates, extremely cautious not to give any occasion for an explosion.

The fruit of Jörgen's best exertions to keep himself unnoticed was nevertheless, as usual, less happy. During the soup he accidentally made a loud noise in eating with his spoon which led to a thundering "Don't slobber like a hog, boy."

After dinner the captain all at once felt the necessity of completing certain computations on a chart and surveying matter that had been left since the autumn.

And now it was not advisable to come too near the office! He had an almost Indian quickness of hearing for the least noise, and was absolutely wild when he was disturbed.

It became quiet, a dead calm over the whole house. The spinning-wheel alone could be heard humming in the sitting-room, and they went gently through the doors below, in genuine terror when in spite of all they creaked or some one happened to let the trap-door into the cellar fall or make the porch door rattle.

How could that foolish Torbjörg hit upon scouring the stairs now? When she hurriedly retreated with her sand and pail, her open mouth and staring eyes showed plainly that she did not comprehend the peculiar inward connection between her scouring and the captain who was sitting safely up there in his office: it was enough that he would fall at once like a tempest down from the upper story.

Now there was a call from up there.

He came out from the office with his drawing-pen in his mouth:

What had become of the old blue portfolio of drawings? It had been lying on the table in the hall upstairs—

Ma must go up, and Thea and Jörgen with her, to be questioned.

There—there on the table—there! it had been lying for five months! Was it the intention to make him entirely miserable with all this putting in order and cleaning?

"But dear, dear Jäger, we shall find it, if you will only have a little patience—if we only look for it."

And there was a search round about everywhere; even in the garret, under old window-panes, and among tables, reels, chests, and old trumpery they ransacked. In his anxious zeal, Jörgen stood on his head, digging deep down into a barrel, when Ma at length sagaciously turned the investigation into the office again. "On top of the cabinet in the office

CHAPTER V

there is a large blue portfolio, but you have looked there, of course."

"There? I — I should like to know who has presumed to —"

He vanished into the office again.

Yes, there it lay.

He flung down his ruling-pen; he really was not in a mood to work any longer! He sat looking gloomily out before him with his elbows leaning against his writing-desk. "It is your fault I say, Ma! — or was it possibly I who had the smart idea of sending her to Ryfylke?" He struck the desk. "It is blood money — blood money, I say! If it is to go on in this way, what shall we have to get Jörgen on with? — Huf, it goes to my head so — eighteen dollars actually thrown into the brook."

"She must have a Sunday dress; Thinka has now worn the clothes she brought from home over a year and a half."

"Even new laced cloth shoes from Stavanger. Yes, indeed, not less than from Stavanger — it is put down so —" he snatched the bill from the desk — "and a patent leather belt, and for half-soling and mending shoes two dollars and a quarter — and then sewing things! I never heard that a young girl in a house bought sewing things — and postage a dollar and a half — it is wholly incredible."

"For the year and a half, you must remember, Jäger, fifteen cents for each letter."

"A miserly judge, I say, who does not even pay for the letters which go from the office! Now, why did she write last when she had just before sent messages in the letter from your sister-in-law? But there it comes with a vengeance — four and a half yards of silk ribbon! Why did n't she make it ten, twenty yards — as long as from here to Ryfylke? Then she might have broken her father at once; for I see what it leads to."

"Remember they go on visits and to parties at the sheriff's, the minister's, and the solicitor's, very often; we must let her go decently dressed."

"Oh, I never heard before that daughters must cost money. It is a brand-new rule you have hit upon; and what is it coming to?"

"He who will not sow, Jäger, shall not reap."

"Yes, don't you think it looks like a fine harvest — this country Adonis there in the office, who casts sheep's eyes at her — a poor clerk who does not have to pass an examination! But he is so quick at the partition of inheritances, ha, ha."

Ma seemed to be a little overcome, and gazed before her hopelessly.

"Ye–es, Thinka wrote that; he is so quick in the partition of inheritances, he is! Don't you think that was rather a nice introduction by her for him?" He hummed. "It is clear as mud that she is taken with him; otherwise your sister-in-law would not have written about it as she did."

CHAPTER V

"Thinka has a gentle nature," came the answer somewhat slowly and thoughtfully, "and is certainly so easily hoodwinked, poor thing, warm and susceptible as she is; but still she has now seen enough of the world about her!"

"Yes, the world does not move in verse! As Lieutenant Bausback said when he paid his debts with old Mother Stenberg; she was exactly three and a half times as old as he when they were married."

"She has always been pliable—we may hope that she is amenable to a word from her parents. I will write and represent to her the prospects."

"The prospects! Don't meddle with that, Ma! Marriages don't grow on trees. Or what kind of a match do you think Thinka can make up here? When I am old and retired on a pension, it is a nice lookout with all our daughters on our hands! Don't let us be mad with pride, Ma, stark mad! That runs in your blood and that of all the Zittows."

Ma's lips stiffened a little and her eyes looked keenly black; but it was over in a moment. "I think that after all we might economize on pork and butter here in the house; it is not half so salt as it is used in many places for servants, and then, when the pigs—only the hams, I mean—can go with the load to the city, then we can very likely find some way to get the money in again. Otherwise, I should be entirely disheartened. But if we are to send the money, I think you ought to send it to the post-office at once, Jäger. They ought not to see anything but that you pay cash down."

The captain rose and puffed. "Ten and five are fifteen—and three are eighteen." He counted the money out of a drawer in his desk. "We shall never see the money again. Where are the scissors, the scissors, I say?"

He began to cut the envelope for the money letter out of an old gray wrapper of an official letter, which he turned.

"Your coat and comforter are lying here, by the stove," said Ma, when she came in again.

"There. Put the sealing-wax and seal in the inside pocket, so that I shall not forget them; otherwise I must pay for sealing."

It was as if the captain's bad humor had been swept away when he came back hastily from the post-office. He had found a letter from Inger-Johanna, and immediately began to peep into it; but it became too dark.

His coat was off in a trice, and, with his hat still on, he began eagerly to read by the newly lighted candle.

"Ma! Ma! Tell Ma to come in at once—and another candle!"

He could not see any more, as the candle made a halo of obscurity, and they had to wait till the wick burned up again.

CHAPTER V

Ma came in, turning down her sleeves after the baking.

"Now you shall hear," he said.

That such a ball cannot last longer! Aunt would like to be one of the first to leave, so during the cotillion I sit in constant anxiety lest she shall order the sleigh. Then I am examined; but then, it is now no longer as it was the first two or three times we drove home, when I chattered and blabbed out every possible thing, turned my soul and all my feelings inside out as a pocket into aunt's bosom.

Yesterday I was at my seventh, and am already engaged way into the ninth; which still will not be my last, I hope, this winter (I led five times). Yesterday, also, I happily escaped Lieutenant Mein, the one with Jörgen's bridle in his mouth, who has begun to want to make sure of me for the cotillion, as he says. He sits and stands in the companies at home at aunt's (which is all he does, as there is not a word in his mouth), and only looks and glowers at me.

Well, you should see my dancing cards! I think I have led a third part of all the dances this winter. Aunt has made me a present of a sash buckle which is beautiful, and, with all the dark yellow stones, improves the dress wonderfully. Aunt has taste; still we never agree when I dress. Old Aunt Alette was up here yesterday, and I got her on my side. So I was relieved from having earrings dangling about my ears; they felt as if two bits of a bridle rein were hanging behind me, and then I must be allowed to have sleeves wide enough to move my arm if I am not to feel like a wooden doll.

You must know that I have grown three inches since I left home. But never in my life have I really known what it is to exist, I believe, till this winter. When I shut my eyes, it is as if I can see in a dream a whole series of balls, with chandeliers under which music is floating, and I am dancing, and am led through the throng, which seems to make way for me.

I understand how Aunt Eleonore must have felt, she who was so beautiful, and whom they say I resemble so; she died after a ball, Aunt Alette says; it must have been of joy. There is nothing like dancing; nothing like seeing them competing for engagements, kneeling, as it were, with their eyes, and then becoming confused when I answer them in the way they don't expect.

And how many times do you really think now I have heard that I have such wonderful black hair, such wonderful firm eyes, such a superb bearing; how many times do you think it has been said in the most delicate manner and in the crudest? Aunt has also begun to admire; I could wish that the whole winter, my whole life (so long as I am beauti-

CHAPTER V

ful, no longer), were one single ball, like the Polish count who drove over sugar.

And then I have always such a desire to die after every time, when I am lying and thinking of it, and, as it were, hear the music in my ears, until I come to think of the next one.

For that I am going to have a new dress, light yellow with black; that and white are most becoming to me, aunt says, and then again, new yellow silk shoes, buttoned up to the ankles; aunt says that my high instep betrays race, and that I feel I have; truly, I don't mind speaking right out what I think; and it is so amusing to see people open their eyes and wonder what sort of a person I am.

I really begin to suspect that several of our gentlemen have never seen a living pig, or a duck, or a colt (which is the prettiest thing I know). They become so stupid as soon as I merely name something from the country; it might be understood if I said it in French—*un canard, un cheval, un cochon, une vache.*

Student Grip contends that of those who have been born in the city not one in ten has ever seen a cow milked. He also provokes aunt by saying that everything which happens in French is so much finer, and thinks that we like to read and cry over two lovers who jump into the water from *Pont Neuf*; but only let the same thing happen here at home, from Vaterland's bridge, then it is vulgar; and indeed I think he is often right. Aunt has to smile. And however much she still says he lacks in polished manners and inborn culture, she is amused at him. And so they are everywhere, for he is invited out every single day in the week.

He generally comes Sunday afternoons and for coffee, for then he is sure that both aunt and I are bored, he says (yes, horribly; now, how can he know that?), and that he is not obliged to walk on stilts, and tell lies among the blue teacups.

And then he and aunt are amusing with a vengeance, when he speaks freely, and aunt opposes him and takes him down. For he thinks for himself always; that I can see when he is sitting with his head on one side and gently stirring his spoon in his cup. It makes one smile, for if he means No, you can see it from the top of his head long before he says it.

He is not a little talked about in the city as one of the worst of the Student Society in being zealous for all their wild ideas. But aunt finds him piquant, and thinks that youth must be suffered to sow its wild oats. On the contrary, uncle says that this kind is more ruinous for a young man's future than the worst transgressions, since it destroys his capacity for discipline.

What he thinks of me I should like to know. Sometimes he asks, impertinently, "You are going to the ball this evening, I suppose, Miss Jäger?"

But I have it out with him to the best of my ability, ask aunt for advice about some fancy work, and yawn so comfortably, and look out of the window just when he is most excited. I see very well it provokes him, and the last time he asked if Miss Jäger would not abstract her thoughts from the next ball for a moment.

Uncle is often cross at his perverseness, and contends that he is a disagreeable person; but I don't believe he would readily let him go from the office, since he is so capable.

Uncle lives only in his work; he is so tremendously noble. You should hear how he can go and worry for the least fault or want of punctuality in his office.

"I think the devil is in the fellow—now he *is* governor," the captain declared. "He has reached the highest grade and can't be removed, and has no need to worry."

"Poor Josiah," sighed Ma, "he was always the most sensitive of my brothers; but the best head."

"Yes, the judge at Ryfylke took both force and will for his part."

. . . .

A fortnight later they were surprised by a letter from the governor's wife, with one from Inger-Johanna enclosed.

The governor's lady must, in any event, be allowed to keep her dear Inger-Johanna at least a year longer; she had become indispensable both to her and the governor, so that it was even difficult for them to realize that she could have another home.

She has spoiled her uncle by the young life she has brought into the house. My dear Zittow with his scrupulous conscientiousness is overburdened with anxieties and responsibilities in his great office, and is sadly in need of amusements and recreation after so many wakeful nights. Nay, so egotistical are we, that I will propose that we divide her in the most unjust manner—that she shall make a visit home this summer, but only to come down to us again. Anything else would be a great disappointment.

But do not let us bring a possibly unnecessary apple of discord upon the carpet too easily; it might turn out like the treaty between the great powers about the beautiful island in the Mediterranean; during the diplomatic negotiations it vanished. And indeed I lack very little of being ready to guarantee that our dear subject of dispute will in a short time herself rule over a home, which will be in proportion to what she with her nature and beauty can lay claim to.

That I, as her aunt, should be somewhat blindly partial to her, I can hardly believe; at least I can cite an experienced, well-informed person of the same mind in our common friend, Captain Rön-

CHAPTER V

now, who last week came here with the royal family from Stockholm, and, in parenthesis be it said —it must be between us —is on the point of having an extraordinary career. He was thoroughly enthusiastic at seeing Inger-Johanna again, and declared that she was a perfect beauty and a born lady, who was sure to excite attention in circles which were even above the common, and much more which we ought not to let our dear child hear. I can only add that on leaving he warmly, and with a certain anxiety, recommended me to keep and still further develop her.

If not just in his first youth, he is at least perhaps *the*, or at any rate one of the, most elegant and most distinguished men in the army, and it would not be difficult for him to win even the most pretentious.

"No, I should say that, by George. Well, Ma," said he, winking, "what do you say now? Now, I think it is all going on well."

The captain took a swinging march over the floor, and then fell upon Inger-Johanna's letter.

Dear Parents,— Now I must tell you something. Captain Rönnow has been here. He came just as aunt had a reception. He looks twice as handsome and brave as he did when he was at our house at Gilje, and I saw plainly that he started a little when he got his eye on me, even while he stopped and paid his respects to aunt.

My heart beat rapidly, you must know, as soon as I saw him again; for I was really half afraid that he would have forgotten me.

But he came up and took both my hands and said very warmly, "The bud which I last saw at Gilje is now blossomed out."

I blushed a little, for I knew very well that it was he who from the first brought it about that I came here.

But I call that finished manners and an easy, straightforward way of conducting himself. Entertaining as he was, he never lost a particle of his grand manly dignity, and there was hardly a question of paying attention to any other person than to him in particular the whole evening. I must admit that hereafter I shall have another standard for a real gentleman whom I would call a man, and there are certainly many who do not come up to it.

Aunt has also expatiated on his manner; I believe she was flattered because he was so kind and cordial to me, she has ever since been in such excellent humor.

After that he was here daily. He had so much to tell us about life in Stockholm and at the court, and always talked to me about you at home, about father, who although he was older—

CHAPTER V

"Much, much older, yes," put in the captain eagerly, "about four or five years, at least."

—always was his never-to-be-forgotten friend.

You can believe those were pleasant evenings. Aunt understands such things. There is a great void since he is gone. Aunt thinks so, too. We have sat talking about him, and hardly anything else than him, these two evenings since he went away.

Yesterday evening Grip came again. We have not seen him at all since the first time Captain Rönnow was here. And can any one imagine such a man? He seems to see nothing in him. He sat and contradicted, and was so cross and disagreeable the whole evening that aunt was quite tired of him. He argued about living externally, hollow drum, and some such things, as if it were not just the genuine manliness and naturalness that one must value so much in Captain Rönnow.

Oh, I lay half the night angry. He sat playing with his teacup and talked about people who could go through the world with a silk ribbon of phrases and compliments: that one could flatter to death a sound understanding, so that at last there was left only a plucked—I plainly heard him mumble—wild goose. Dreadful insolence! I am sure he meant me.

When he had gone aunt also said that hereafter she should refuse to receive him, when there was no other company present; she was tired of his performances *en tête-à-tête;* that sort of men must have a certain restraint put upon them. He will never have any kind of a career, she thought, he carries his own notions too high.

However, it will be very tiresome if he stays away; for with all his peculiarities he is very often a good war comrade for me against aunt.

Chapter VI

THE captain had kept the cover of his old large meerschaum pipe polished with chalk for three days, without being willing to take it down from the shelf; he had trimmed and put in new mouthpieces, and held a feast of purification on the remainder, as well as on all the contents of the tobacco table, the ash receiver, the tobacco stems, and lava-like scrapings from the pipe. He had let the sexton do his best at tuning the clavichord, and put two seats, painted white, on the stoop. The constantly neglected lattice-work around the garden now glistened here and there with fresh white palings, like single new teeth which are stuck between a whole row of old gray ones. The walks in the garden must be swept and garnished, the yard was cleaned up, and, finally, the cover put on the well, which was to have been done all the years when the children were small.

It was the captain who, in an almost vociferous good humor, was zealously on the move everywhere.

Sometimes he took a kind of rest and stood puffing on the steps or in the window of the large room which looked down toward the country highway; or in the shades of the evening he took a little turn down to the gate and sat there on the stone fence with his pipe. If any one passed by going south, he would say, "Are you going to the store to buy a plug of tobacco, Lars? If you meet a fine young lady in a cariole, greet her from the captain at Gilje; it is my daughter who is coming from the city."

If the person was some poor old crone of the other sex, to her astonishment a copper coin fell down on the road before her: "There, Kari; there, Siri: you may want something to order a crutch carriage with."

A surprise which was so much the greater as the captain at other times cherished a genuine liking for flaying old beggar women. The whole stock of tempestuous oaths and of abusive words coined in the inspiration of the moment, which was in his blood from the drill-ground and military life, must now and then have an outbreak. The old women who went on crutches were long accustomed to this treatment, and knew what to expect when they were going away from the house, after having first got a good load in their bags in the kitchen. It was like a tattoo about their ears, accompanied by Pasop's wild barking.

But in these days, while he was going about in joyful expectation and awaiting his daughter's return home, he was what made him a popular man both in the district and among his men, straightforward and sportive, something of the old gay Peter Jäger.

CHAPTER VI

The captain had just been in again in the afternoon and tried the concert pitch on the clavichord, which was constantly lowering, and compared his deep bass with its almost soundless rumbling G, when Jörgen thought he saw, through the window, a movable spot on one of the light bits of the highway, which was visible even on the other side of the lake.

The captain caught up his field-glasses, rushed out on the steps and in again, called to Ma—and afterwards patiently took his post at the open window, while he called Ma in again every time they came into the turns.

Down there it did not go so quickly. Svarten stopped of his own accord at every man he met on the way; and then Great-Ola must explain.

A young lady with a duster tightly fastened about her waist, parasol and gloves, and such a fine brass-bound English trunk on the back of the cariole, was in itself no common thing. But that it was the daughter of the captain at Gilje who was coming home raised the affair up to the sensational, and the news was therefore well spread over the region when, toward evening, the cariole had got as far as the door at home.

There stood mother and father and Jörgen and Thea and the sub-officer, Tronberg, with his small bag yonder at the corner of the house, and the farm-hands and girls inside the passageway—and Great-

Ola was cheated out of lifting the young lady down on the steps, for she herself jumped from the cariole step straight into the arms of her father, and then kissed her mother and hugged Thea and pulled Jörgen by the hair a little forced dance around on the stairs, so that he should feel the first impression of her return home.

Yes, it was the parasol she had lost on the steps and which a bare-footed girl came up with; Ma had a careful eye upon it—the costly, delicate, fringed parasol with long ivory handle had been lying there between the steps and the cariole wheel.

The captain took off her duster himself—The hair, the dress, the gloves; that was the way she looked, a fine grown lady from head to foot.

And so they had the Gilje sun in the room!

"I have been sitting and longing all day for the smell of the *petum* and to see a little cloud of smoke about your head, father—I think you are a little stouter—and then your dress-coat—I always thought of you in the old shiny one. And mother —and mother!" She rushed out after her into the pantry, where she stayed a long time.

Then she came out more quietly.

A hot fire was blazing in the kitchen. There stood Marit, a short, red-cheeked mountain girl, with white teeth and small hands, stirring the porridge so that the sweat dropped from her face; she knew very well that Great-Ola would have it so that fifteen

CHAPTER VI

men could dance on the surface, and now she got the help of the young lady. After that Inger-Johanna must over and spin on Torbjörg's spinning-wheel.

The captain only went with her and looked on with half moistened eyes, and when they came in again Inger-Johanna got the bottle from the sideboard, and gave each of them out there a dram in honor of her return.

The supper-table was waiting in the sitting-room on a freshly laid cloth — red mountain trout and her favorite dish, strawberries and cream.

They must not think of waking her, so tired as she was last night, father had said.

And therefore Thea had sat outside of the threshold from half-past six, waiting to hear any noise, so that she could rush in with the tray and little cakes, for Inger-Johanna was to have her coffee in bed.

Jörgen kept her company, taken up with studying the singular lock on her trunk, and then with scanning the light, delicate patent leather shoes. He rubbed them on his forehead and his nose, after having moistened them with his breath.

Now she was waking up in there, and open flew the door for Jörgen, Thea, and Pasop, and afterwards Torbjörg with the cup of coffee.

Yes, she was at home now.

The fragrance of the hay came in through the

open window, and she heard them driving the rumbling loads into the barn.

And when she saw, from the window, the long narrow lake in the valley down below, and all the mountain peaks which lifted themselves so precipitously up towards the heavens over the light fog on the other side, she understood some of her mother's feeling that here it was cramped, and that it was two hundred long miles to the city. But then it was so fragrant and beautiful—and then, she was really home at Gilje.

She must go out and lie in the hay, and let Jörgen hold the buck that was inclined to butt, so she could get past, and then look at his workshop and the secret hunting gun he was making out of the barrel and lock of an old army gun.

It was a special confidence to his grown-up sister, for powder and gun were most strictly forbidden him, which did not prevent his having his arsenals of his father's coarse-grained cartridge powder hidden in various places in the hills.

And then she must be with Thea and find out all about the garden, and with her father on his walks here and there; they went up by the cow-path, with its waving ferns, white birch stems, and green leaves, over the whole of the sloping ridge of Gilje.

It was like a happy, almost giddy, intoxication of home-coming for three or four days.

CHAPTER VI

It came to be more like every-day life, when Ma began to talk about this and that of the household affairs and to make Inger-Johanna take part in her different cares and troubles.

What should be done with Jörgen? They must think of having him go to the city soon. Ma had thought a good deal about writing to Aunt Alette and consulting with her. Father must not be frightened about spending too much money. If Aunt Alette should conclude to take him to board, then it would n't involve the terrible immediate outlay of money. They could send many kinds of provisions there, butter and cheese, *fladbröd*, dried meat, and bacon as often as there was an opportunity.

She must talk with father about this sometime later in the winter, when she had heard what Aunt Alette thought.

And with Thinka they had gone through a great deal. Ma had had all she could do to keep father out of it — you know how little he can bear annoyances — and she had found it a matter almost of life and death on Wednesdays to intercept Jörgen, when he brought the mail, to get hold of Thinka's letters. This spring Ma had written time after time, and represented to her what kind of a future she was preparing for herself, if she, in weakness and folly, gave way to her rash feelings for this clerk, Aas.

But in the beginning, you see, there came some

letters back, which were very melancholy. One could live even in poorer circumstances, she wrote,—it seems that there was a rather doubtful prospect of his getting a situation as a country bailiff that she had set her hopes on.

Ma had placed it seriously before her how such a thing as that might end. Suppose he was sick or died, where would she and perhaps a whole flock of children take refuge?

"It depends on overcoming the first emotion of the fancy. Now she is coming home in the autumn, and it could be wished that she had gotten over her feelings. My brother Birger is so headstrong; but maybe it was for the best that, as my sister-in-law writes, as soon as he got a hint of the state of affairs, he gave Aas his dismissal and sent him packing that very day. The last two or three letters show that Thinka is quieter."

"Thinka is horribly meek," exclaimed Inger-Johanna with flashing eyes. "I believe they could pickle her and put her down and tie up the jar; she would not grumble. If Uncle Birger had done so to me, I would not have stayed there a day longer."

"Inger-Johanna! Inger-Johanna!" Ma shook her head. "You have a dangerous, spoiled temper. It is only the very, very smallest number of us women who are able to do what they would like to."

The captain did not disdain the slightest occasion

to bring forward his daughter just come home from the city.

He had turned the time to account, for in the beginning of the next week he would be obliged to go on various surveys up on the common land and then to the drills.

They had made a trip down to the central part of the district, to Pastor Horn's, and on the way stopped and called on Sexton Semmelinge and Bardon Kleven, the bailiff. They had been to Dr. Bauman, the doctor of the district; and now on Sunday they were invited to Sheriff Gülcke's—a journey of thirty-five miles down the valley.

It was an old house of a *calêche*, repaired a hundred times, which was drawn out of its hiding-place, and within whose chained together arms Svarten and the dun horse—the blind bay had long since been sent away—were to continue their three-months-long attempt to agree in the stall.

If the beasts had any conception, it must most likely have been that it was an enormously heavy plough they were drawing, in a lather, up and down hill, with continual stoppings to get breath and let those who were sitting in it get in and out.

If there was anything the captain adhered to, it was military punctuality, and at half-past four in the morning the whole family in full dress, the captain and Jörgen with their pantaloons turned up, the ladies with their dresses tucked up, were wandering on foot down the Gilje hills—they were some of the worst on the whole road—while Great-Ola drove the empty carriage down to the highway.

The dun horse was better fitted for pulling than holding back, so that it was Svarten that must be depended on in the hills, and Great-Ola, the captain, and Jörgen must help.

It was an exceedingly warm day, and the carriage rolled on in an incessant dense, stifling dust of the road about the feet of the horses and the wheels. But then it was mainly down hill, and they rested and got breath every mile.

At half-past one they had only to cross the ferry and a short distance on the other side again up to the sheriff's farm.

On the ferry a little toilet was temporarily made, and the captain took his new uniform coat out of the carriage box and put it on. Except that Jörgen had greased his pantaloons from the wheels, not a single accident had happened on the whole trip.

As soon as they came up on the hill, they saw the judge's carriage roll up before them through the gate, and in the yard they recognized the doctor's cariole and the lawyer's gig. There stood the sheriff himself, helping the judge's wife out of the carriage; his chief clerk and his daughters were on the steps.

So far as the ladies were concerned, there must, of course, be a final toilet and a change of clothes before they found themselves presentable. One of

CHAPTER VI

the two daughters of the lawyer was in a red and the other in a clear white dress, and of the three daughters of the judge, two were in white and one in blue.

That a captain's daughter, with his small salary, came in brown silk with patent leather shoes, could only be explained by the special circumstances, suggested Mrs. Scharfenberg in the ear of old Miss Horn of the parsonage; it was, in all probability, one of the governor's lady's, which had been made over down in the city.

The fact was that young Horn who, it was expected, would be chaplain to his father, the minister, treated Inger-Johanna in a much more complimentary manner than he showed toward Mrs. Scharfenberg's daughter, Bine, to whom he was as good as engaged; and the chief clerk did not seem to be blind to her. They both ran to get a chair for her.

The sofa was assigned to the judge's wife and to Ma, as a matter of course. Mrs. Scharfenberg did not think this quite right either, since her husband had been nominated second for the judgeship of Sogn; and that the sheriff had to-day also invited the rich Mrs. Silje was, her husband said, only a bid for popularity: she was still always what she was—widow of the country storekeeper, Silje.

It was a long time to sit and exchange compliments, before the mainstay of the dinner, the sheriff's roast, was sufficiently and thoroughly done, and he got a nod from his wife to ask the company out to the table in the large room.

The only one who laughed and talked before the ice was fairly broken was Inger-Johanna, who chatted with the judge and then with Horn and the army doctor.

Ma pursed her lips a little uneasily, as she sat on the sofa and pretended to be absorbed in conversation with Mrs. Brinkman; she knew what they all would say about her afterwards.

It had been a rather warm dinner. Through the abundant provision of the sheriff, the fatigue and hunger after the journey had given place to an extremely lively mood spiced with speeches and songs.

They had sat a long time at the table before the scraping of the judge's chair finally gave the signal for the breaking up.

The sheriff now stood stout and beaming during the thanks for the meal, and demanded and received his tribute as host—a kiss from each one of the young ladies.

The masculine part of the company distributed themselves with their coffee-cups out in the cool hall and on the stairs, or went with their tobacco pipes into the yard, while the ladies sat around the coffee-table in the parlor.

The judge talked somewhat loudly with the sher-

CHAPTER VI

iff, and the captain, red and hot, stood a little way out in the yard, cooling himself.

The doctor came up and clapped him on the shoulder. "The sheriff really took the spigot out of the bung to-day: we had excellent drink."

"Oh, if one only had a pipe now, and could go and loaf."

"You have got one in your hand, man."

"Really? But filled, you see."

"You just went in and filled it."

"I? No, really; but a light, you see, a light."

"I say, Jäger, Scharfenberg is already up taking a nap."

"Yes, yes; but the bay, you cheated me shamefully in that."

"Oh, nonsense, Peter; your cribber ate himself half out of my stall—That Madeira was strong."

" Rist—my daughter, Inger-Johanna —"

"Yes, you see, Peter, I forgive you that you are a little cracked about her; she may make stronger heads than yours whirl round."

"She is beautiful—beautiful." His voice was assuming an expression of serious pathos.

The two military men, at a sedate, thoughtful pace, walked back to one of the sleeping-rooms in the second story.

In the hall, tall Buchholtz, the judge's chief clerk, was standing, stiff and silent, against the wall, with his coffee-cup in his hand; he was pondering whether anyone would notice anything wrong about him. He had been in the coffee room with the ladies and tried to open a conversation with Miss Jäger.

"Have you been here long, Miss Jäger?"

"Three weeks."

"How lo–ong do you intend to stay here?"

"Till the end of August."

"Don't you miss the city u–p here?"

"No, not at all."

She turned from him, and began to talk with her mother. The same questions had now been asked her by all the gentlemen.

The irreproachable Candidate Horn stood by the door enjoying his coffee and the defeat of the chief clerk. He was lying in wait for an opportunity to have a chat with Inger-Johanna, but found an insurmountable obstacle in the judge's well-read wife, who began to talk with her about French literature, a region in which he felt he could not assert himself.

At the request of the sheriff, a general exit took place later. The ladies must go out on the porch and see the young people playing "the widower seeking a mate."

Mrs. Silje sat there, broad and good-natured after all the good eating, and enjoyed it.

"No, but he did not catch her this time, no. Make the strap around your waist tighter, next

CHAPTER VI

time, sir!" She smiled when the chief clerk's attempt to catch Inger-Johanna failed; "she is such a fine young lady to try for."

Mrs. Scharfenberg found that there was a draught on the stairs, and as she moved into the hall, where the sheriff's wife, always an invalid, sat wrapped up in her shawl, she could not but say to her and the judge's wife that the young lady's reckless manner of running—so that you could even see the stockings above her shoes—smacked rather much of being free. But she was sure Mrs. Silje did not find it in the least unbecoming. She remarked sharply, "She had herself gone so many times on the sunny hillside with the other girls, raking hay in her smock before she was married to the trader."

Ma, indeed, gave Inger-Johanna an anxious hint as soon as she could reach her.

"You must not run so violently, child. It does not look well—you must let yourself be caught."

"By that chief clerk—never!"

Ma sighed.

They kept on with the game till tea time, when those who had been missing after dinner again showed themselves in a rested condition, ready to begin a game of Boston for the evening.

"But Jörgen—where is Jörgen?"

In obedience to the call, somewhat pale and in a cold perspiration, but with a bold front, he came down from the office building, where he had been sitting, smoking tobacco on the sly with the sheriff's clerk and "the execution horse," whose racy designation was due to his unpopular portion of the sheriff's functions.

The game of Boston was continued after supper with violent defeats and quite wonderful exposed hands, between the judge, the captain, the sheriff, and the attorney.

In the other room Ma sat uneasy, wondering when father would think of breaking up—they had a very long journey home, and it was already ten o'clock. The sheriff had urged them in vain to remain all night; but it didn't answer this time; Jäger had definite reasons why they must be home again to-morrow.

She sat in silence, resting her hopes on the sharp little Mrs. Scharfenberg, trusting she would soon dare to show herself in the door of the card room.

But it dragged on; the other ladies were certainly resting their hope on her.

She nodded to Inger-Johanna. "Can't you go in," she whispered, "and remind your father a little of the time—but only as if of your own accord?"

Finally at eleven o'clock they were sitting in the carriage—after the sheriff had again asserted, on the steps, his privilege of an old man towards the young ladies. He was a real master in meeting all the playful ways they had of escaping in order to be saved from the smacking good-by.

CHAPTER VI

The chief clerk and Candidate Horn went with the carriage to the gate.

"It was neither for your sake nor mine, Ma," said the captain.

He was driving, but turned incessantly in order to hear the talk in the carriage, and throw in an observation with it. Jörgen and Thea, who had kept modestly quiet the whole day, but had made many observations, nevertheless, were now on a high horse; Thea especially plumed herself as the only soul who had succeeded in escaping the sheriff.

And now they were on the way home in the light, quiet July night, up hill and up hill—in places down, foot by foot, step by step, except where they dared to let the carriage go faster as they came to the bottom of a hill.

A good level mile or two, where they could all sit in the carriage, was passed over at a gentle jog-trot. It was sultry with a slightly moist fragrance from the hay-cocks, and a slight impression of twilight over the land—Great-Ola yawned, the captain yawned, the horses yawned, Jörgen nodded, Thea slept, wrapped up under Ma's shawl. Now and then they were roused by the rushing of a mountain brook, as it flowed foaming under a bridge in the road.

Inger-Johanna sat dreaming, and at last saw a yellowish brown toad before her, with small, curious eyes and a great mouth—and then it rose up, so puffed up and ungainly, and hopped down towards her.

The horses stopped.

"Oh, I believe I was dreaming about the sheriff!" said Inger-Johanna, as she woke up shivering.

"We must get out here," came sleepily from the captain, "on the Rognerud hills; Ma can stay in with Thea."

The day was beginning to dawn. They saw the sun bathe the mountain-tops in gold and the light creep down the slopes. The sun lay as it were still, and peeped at them first, till it at once bounded over the crest in the east like a golden ball, and colored red the wooded mountain sides and hills on the west side, clear down to the greensward shining with dew.

Still they toiled, foot by foot, up the hills.

On the Gilje lands the people had already been a long time at work spreading out the hay, when they saw them coming.

"It is good to be home again," declared Ma. "I wonder if Marit has remembered to hang the trout in the smoke."

Marit came rushing out of the door of the porch: "There was a fine city traveller came this way last night! He who was here two years ago, and had his shoes mended. I did not know anything better than to let him sleep in the blue chamber."

CHAPTER VI

"Oh, ho! Student Grip! I suppose he is on his way towards home."

Ma looked at once at Inger-Johanna; she fell into a reverie. She stepped hurriedly out of the carriage.

"Jäger is going surveying to-morrow a long distance into the mountains,—clear over to the Grönnelid *saeters*," Ma said to him, when he came out of his room in the morning, "and there is so much that must be done."

"So—oh—and to-morrow early." The student hesitated. "My plan is to go home over the mountain, as I did last time—to get a little really fresh air, away from the stuffy town air and the law-books."

"But then you could go with Jäger? It will be thirty-five to forty miles you could go together up in the mountains—and for Jäger, it would be a real pleasure to have company. You won't have any objection, I suppose, to my putting up something for you to eat by the way?"

"Thanks—I thank you very much for all your kindness."

"She will not have me, that is plain," he muttered, while he wandered about the yard during the forenoon; they were all asleep except the mistress. But he did not come here to escort the captain.

In the afternoon, when it began to grow a little cool, the captain, Inger-Johanna, Jörgen, and

Student Grip took the lonely road to the mill. Great-Ola and Aslak, the crofter, went with them —something was to be done to the mill-wheel, now that the stream was almost dry.

They stood there studying eagerly how the wheel could best be raised off the axis.

"That Jörgen, that Jörgen, he has got the hang of the wheel!" exclaimed the captain. "You can get Tore, the joiner, to help, Ola, as soon as you come back with the horses from the mountain—and let Jörgen show you how: he understands it, he does—if it is only not a book, he is clever enough."

"You will have to take hold of your forelock and try and cram, Jörgen; do as you did with the rye-pudding—the sooner it is eaten, the sooner it is over," said Grip, to comfort him.

"Look here, I came near forgetting the fish-lines for to-morrow. You will have to go down to the store this evening, Jörgen. We catch the trout ourselves up there, as you will see," said the captain, turning to Grip.

"Oh—oh—yes," he puffed, while they were sauntering toward home together. "I certainly need to go to the mountains now, I always come down again three or four pounds lighter."

"I have wandered about that part of the country from the time I was a schoolboy," remarked Grip. "We must put Lake Bygdin into the geography

CHAPTER VI

—that it was discovered only a few years ago, in the middle of a broad mountain plateau, which only some reindeer hunter or other knew anything about."

"Not laid down on any map, no—as blank as in the interior of Africa, marked out as unexplored," the captain pointed out. "But then there is traffic going on between the districts, both of people and cattle, and the mountains have their names from ancient times down among the common people."

"True, the natives also knew the interior of Africa, but on that account it is not called discovered by the civilized world," said Grip, smiling. "I always wondered what could be found in such a mysterious region in the middle of the country. There might be a great deal there: valleys entirely deserted from ancient times—old, sunken timber halls, and then wild reindeer rushing here and there over the wastes."

"Yes, shooting," agreed the captain; "we get many a tender reindeer steak from over there."

"It was that which attracted me, when I met the reindeer hunter two years ago: I wanted to explore a little, to see what there was there."

"Exactly like all that we imagined about the city," exclaimed Inger-Johanna.

"You ought to go with your father part of the way over the mountains, Miss Inger-Johanna—see if you could find some lofty bower."

"That is an idea, not at all stupid," broke in the captain, "not impossible, not at all! You could ride all the way to the Grönnelid *saeters*."

"Ah, if you could carry that through, father!" she exclaimed earnestly. "Now I have also taken a fancy to see what there is there—I believe we always thought the world ended over there at our own *saeter* pastures."

"I have some blankets on the pack-saddle, and where they can get a roof over my head there will be room enough for you too.—Come, come, Morten, will you let people alone!" The captain took out a roll of tobacco and held a piece out to the stable goat, that was coming, leaping, towards them from the yard. "There, mumble-beard—he will have his allowance, the rascal.—Ma," he called, when he saw her coming from the storehouse, "what would you say if I should take Inger-Johanna with me to-morrow? Then they will have company home on Friday with Ola and the horses—she and Jörgen."

"But, dear Jäger, why should she go up there?"

"She can pass the night at Grönnelid *saeter*."

"Such a fatiguing trip! It is absolutely without a path and wild where you must go."

"She can ride the horse a good ways beyond the *saeter*. Svarten will go as steady as a minister with her and the pack-saddle—both on the mountain and in the bog. I will take the dun horse myself."

CHAPTER VI

He had become very eager at the prospect of taking her with him. "Certainly, you shall go. You must put a good lot in the provision bag, Ma. We must be off early to-morrow at five o'clock. Tronberg will join us with a horse farther up, so there will be a way of giving you a mount also, Grip."

Grip started on a run with Jörgen towards the yard, finally caught him, and drove him in through the open kitchen window.

The captain, with his neck burned brown, toiled, red and sweating in his shirt-sleeves, in the mountain fields up under Torsknut.

The packhorses went first with Inger-Johanna and all the equipment, and by the side of the captain walked some farmers who carried their coats on sticks over their shoulders on account of the heat, and eagerly pointed out bounds and marks, every time they stopped and he was to draw some line or other as a possible connection.

They had passed the night at the Grönnelid *saeters* and been out on the moors making a sketch survey at five o'clock in the morning, had ridden over flat mountain wastes among willow thickets, while the horses, step by step, waded across windings of the same river.

Now they stopped again after a steep ascent to wait for Tronberg, whom they had seen below on the hills.

The captain took out his spy-glass, and after a cursory glance over the shining icy fields which lay like a distant sea of milk, turned it farther and farther down.

The perspiration rolled in great drops off his forehead and eyelids, so that the glass was blurred, and he was obliged to wipe it again with his large, worn silk handkerchief.

Then he rested the spy-glass on the back of the packhorse, and held it still a long time. "That must be the Rognelid folk, after all, who are moving there west of Braekstad heights. What do you say?"

The people to whom he turned needed only to shade their eyes to agree with him that it was the opposite party whom they were to meet the next morning at Lake Tiske. But they were too polite fellows to express it otherwise than by saying in a flattering manner, "What a spy-glass the captain has!"

During this surveying business he was borne, so to speak, on a royal cushion by the anxious interests of both parties to the contest; it contributed to the pleasure he took in his trips in the mountains in summer to feel himself in that way lifted up by their hands.

"Have you been fishing, Tronberg?" he shouted when the head of the subaltern's "Rauen" appeared nodding down in the steep path. "Trout! Caught to-day?"

"This morning, Captain."

CHAPTER VI

The captain took up the string and looked at the gills. "Yes, they are to-day's."

The subaltern took off his hat, and dried his forehead and head. "One could easily have fried the fish on the rocky wall in the whole of that pan of a valley over there that I came through," Tronberg said.

"Fine fish. See that, Grip,—weighs at least three pounds."

"Goodness sake, the young lady here!" exclaimed the subaltern, involuntarily bringing himself up to a salute when Inger-Johanna turned her horse round and looked at the shiny speckled fish which hung on the pack-saddle.

But old Lars Opidalen, the one who had asked for the survey, gently passed his coarse hand over hers, while he counted the trout on the willow branch. "Can such also be of the earth?" he said, quietly wondering.

"Help the young lady, Lars, while she dismounts: it is not well to ride any longer on this smooth bare rock."

The path ascended, steeper and steeper, with occasional marshy breathing places in between — it was often entirely lost in the gray mountain.

The mournful cry of a fish eagle sounded over them. It circled around, cried, and went off when Jörgen shouted at it. It must have had a nest somewhere up on that rocky wall.

The captain's shotgun was brought out, and Tronberg attempted a shot, but could not get within range. If he could only lie in wait for it behind the great stones up here!

The eagle whirled around again near them with broad, outspread wings.

Suddenly there was a report up above on the slope strewn with stones, and the eagle made some vigorous, flapping strokes with its wings; it struggled so as not to fall down.

The shot had gone through one wing, so that daylight could be seen through the hole in the feathers. The bird evidently found it difficult to preserve its equilibrium.

"What a shame!—it is wounded," exclaimed Inger-Johanna.

"Who shot?" demanded the captain, taken aback.

"Jörgen ran off with the rifle," Tronberg replied.

"Jörgen! He can't make me believe it was his first shot, the rogue! But he shot himself free from a thrashing that time—for it was a good shot, Tronberg. The rascal! He has been most strictly forbidden to meddle with guns."

"Forbidden indeed," murmured Grip. "Is it not remarkable, Miss Inger-Johanna, it is always the forbidden thing in which we are most skilful? It is exactly these prohibitions that constitute our most potent education—But that is going the way of villains in growth, and leaves its marks behind—makes men with good heads but bad characters."

Grip and Inger-Johanna walked ahead with the horses. A strange, hazy warm smoke lay below over the marshes in the afternoon: it veiled the lines there. Up here on the mountain the air was so sparkling clear.

Foot by foot, the animals picked their way over the piles of stony débris between the enormous fallen masses which lay, scattered here and there, like moss-covered gray houses, with now and then a fairy forelock of dwarf birch upon them, while on the mountain ledges still hung yellow tufts of saxifrage.

"Only see all this warped, twisted, fairy creation. You could say that life is really turned to stone here, —and yet it bubbles up."

He stopped. "Do you know what I could wish, Miss Inger-Johanna?" There was no longer any trace of the strain of irony which usually possessed him. "Simply to be a schoolmaster!—teach the children to lay the first two sticks across by their own plain thoughts. It is the fundamental logs that are laid the wrong way in us. They ought to be allowed to believe just as much and as little as they could really swallow. And to the door with the whole host of these cherished, satisfactory prohibitions! I should only show the results—mix powder and matches together before their eyes till it went into the air, and then say, 'If you please,

Jörgen, so far as I am concerned, you can go with the two things in your pocket as much as you like: it is you, yourself, who will be blown into the air.' It is the sense of responsibility that is to be cultivated while the boy is growing up, if he is to be made a man."

"You have an awful lot of ideas, Grip."

"Crotchets, you mean? If I had any talent with the pen,—but I am so totally dependent on word of mouth. You see, there are only four doors, and they are called theology, philology, medicine, and law, and I have temporarily knocked at the last. What I want there, I don't know. Have you heard of the cat which they put into a glass ball and pumped the air out? It noticed that there was something wrong. It was troubled for breath; the air was constantly getting thinner and thinner; and so it put one paw on the hole. I shall also allow myself to put one paw on the draught hole—for here is a vacuum—not up in the skies with the poets, of course. There it lightens and shines, and they write about working for the people and for freedom and for everything lofty and great in as many directions as there are points on a compass—but in reality, down on the earth—for a prosaic person who would take hold and set in motion a little of the phrases—there it is entirely closed. There is no use for all our best thoughts and ideas in the practical world, I can tell you; not even so much

CHAPTER VI

that a man can manage to make himself unhappy in them.

"And so one lives as best he can his other life with his comrades, and re-baptizes himself in punch with them every time he has been really untrue to himself in the tea parties. But taste this air — every blessed breath like a glass of the finest, finest — nay, what shall I call it?"

"Punch," was the rather short answer.

"No, life! With this free nature one does not feel incited to dispute. I am in harmony with the mountain, with the sun, with all these crooked tough birch-osiers. If people down there only were themselves! But that they never are, except in a good wet party when they have got themselves sufficiently elevated from the bottom of the well. There exists a whole freemasonry, the members of which do not know each other except in that form, or else in Westerman's steam baths when Westerman whips us with fresh birch leaves in a temperature of eighty degrees. The bath-house was our fathers' national club, did you know that?"

"No, indeed; I am learning a great many new things, I think," she said, with half concealed humor.

" Listen, listen! The golden plover whistling," whispered Jörgen.

The sound came from a little marshy spot which was white with cotton grass.

They stood listening.

"Did you ever hear anything so tremendously quiet," said Grip, "after a single little peep. There are such peeps here and there in the country. Abel, he died, he did—of what? Of drink, they said"—he shook his head—"of vacuum."

He was walking in his shirt-sleeves, and flung the willow stick, which he had broken off while he was talking, far down over the rocky incline.

"There, Captain, see the line, as it has been from ancient times for Opidalen," shouted old Lars—"straight, straight along by the Notch, where we shall go down and across the lake—straight toward Rödkampen on Torsknut—there where you see the three green islands under the rocks, Captain." He shook his stick in his eagerness. "For that I shall bring witnesses—and if they were all living here who have fished on our rights in the lake, both in my father's and grandfather's time, there would be a crowd of people against their villainies in Rognelien."

The afternoon shadows fell into the Notch, where the ice-water trickled down through the cracks in the black mountain wall. Here and there the sun still shone on patches of greenish yellow reindeer moss, on some violet, white, or yellow little clusters of high mountain flowers, which exemplified the miracle of living their tinted life of beauty up here close to the snow.

CHAPTER VI

"There comes Mathis with the boat," exclaimed old Lars.

The boat, which was to carry them over to the shelter, crept like an insect far below them on the green mirror of the lake.

The going down was real recreation for the captain's rather stout body, short of breath as he was, and the prospect of being able to indulge in his favorite sport, fishing, contributed greatly to enlivening his temper.

"We are coming here just at the right time: they will bite," he suggested.

When they embarked in the square trough, which was waiting for them down by the fishing-hut, he had the line ready. He had already, with great activity, taken care of the bait, carried in a goat's horn.

Those of the train who could not be accommodated in the boat went around the lake with the horses. They saw them now and then on the crags, while they rowed out.

"What do you say to a trial along the shore there in the shade, Mathis? Don't you think they will take the hook there?—We are not rowing so straight over at once, I think," said the captain slyly.

Under the thwarts Mathis's own line was lying; and Inger-Johanna also wanted to try her hand at it.

The captain put the bait on for her. But she would not sit and wait till they reached the fishing place; she threw the line out at once and let it trail behind the boat, while, as they rowed, she, off and on, gave a strong pull at it.

"See how handy she is," exclaimed the captain; "it is inborn — you come from a race of fishermen, for I was brought up in the Bergen district, and my father before me. If I had a dollar for every codfish I have pulled out of Alverströmmen, there would be something worth inheriting from me — What! what!"

A swirl was heard far behind in the wake. Inger-Johanna gave a vigorous pull; the yellow belly of a fish appeared a moment in the sunlight above the surface of the water.

She continued, after the first feverish jerk upon the line, in a half risen position, to pull it in.

When she lifted the shining fish high upon the edge of the boat, she burst out into a triumphant cry, "The first fish I have ever caught!"

Grip took the fish off the hook, and threw it far off. "Then it shall also be allowed to keep its life!"

The captain angrily moved his heavy body, so that it shook the boat. But that the ill-timed offering to the deep was made for the honor of the apple of his eye greatly mitigated the stupidity.

And when they got in under the knoll, where he cast his line, he suddenly sang a verse from his youthful recollections of the Bergen quarter, which had slumbered in him for many a long year.

CHAPTER VI

I lay basking in the sun,
While the boat was drifting in the current,
I heard the sillock and climbed into the top,
I was giddy with my dream.
I awoke wet through,
And the thwart was floating,
While the boat was drifting in the current.

His deep bass came out with full force in the silence under the knoll.

The lake was like a mirror, and the captain took one trout after another.

Torsknut, with patches and fields of snow on the summit, stood on its head deep down below them, so that it almost caused a giddy feeling when they looked out over the boat-rail. And when they arrived under the cattle station, the steep green mountain side, with all the grazing cattle, was reproduced so clearly that they could count the horns in the water.

"Nay, here the cows walk like flies on the wall," said the captain. "If the milk-bucket falls up there, it will roll down to us into the boat."

The shelter was, in fact, nothing more than a little mud hut on the rocky slope, and a little wooden shed, with boulders on the roof, and a hole in it. There the captain was to be quartered, and Inger-Johanna was to sleep till the sun rose, and she, with Jörgen, Great-Ola, and Svarten, should go back again to the Grönnelid *saeters*.

They had eaten supper—the trout and an improvised cream porridge—and were now standing, watching the sun set behind the great mountains.

The captain was going about on the turf, in slippers and unbuttoned uniform coat, smoking his pipe with extreme satisfaction. He stopped now and then and gazed at the sun playing on the mountain peaks far away.

Then a range of hitherto dark blue peaks took fire in violet blushing tints, until they seemed an entire glowing flame. And now the snow-fields became rose-red in the east—wonderful fairy tales in towers and castles gleamed there—the three snowy peaks then were turned to blood, with a burning, shining flash on top of the middle one. And again in the distance, still unlighted, blue peaks, snow-drifts, and glens, on which the shadows were playing.

Jörgen was lying, with his father's spy-glass, watching the reindeer on the ice-fields.

"Good-by, Miss Inger-Johanna," said Grip. "I am going over the mountains to-night, with one of the men to guide me. There are more people here than the hut will accommodate. But first let me say to you," he added in a subdued tone, "that this open-hearted day on the high mountain has been one of the few of my life. . . . I have not found it necessary to say a single cowardly, bad witticism—nor to despise myself," he added roughly. "Yes, just so—just as you stand there, so fine and

CHAPTER VI

erect and haughty, under the great straw hat, I shall remember you till we meet in the city again."

"It is a good ten miles to Svartdalsbod," suggested the captain, when he took leave—"always welcome to Gilje, Grip."

He was already giving his farewell greetings a good distance up the steep ascent of Torsknut.

"Does not seem to know fatigue, that fellow," said the captain.

She stood looking at him. The last rays of the sun cast a pale yellow tinge in the evening with this transparent mirroring. There was such a warm life in her face!

Some kind of an insect—a humble-bee or a wasp—buzzed through the open window into the room newly tinted in blue—hummed so noisily on the window-pane that the young girl with the luxuriant black hair and the slightly dark, clear-cut face, who was lying sleeping into the morning, was almost aroused.

She lay sound asleep on her side, after having come home in the night. The impressions of the mountains' summits were still playing in her brain. She had another trout on the line—it flashed and floundered there in the lake—Grip came up with two sticks, which were to be placed crossways.

Surr-humm! straight into her face, so that she woke up.

The day was already far advanced.

There on the toilet table with white hangings above it surrounding the glass which had been put there for her return home, was the violet soap in silver paper.

It was plainly that which attracted all the inexperienced insects to ruin: they had found the way to an entirely new world of flowers there and plunged blindly headlong, believing in the discovery, without any conception of the numerous artificial products of the age outside of the mountain region—that the fragrance of violets did not produce violets, but only horrid, horrid pains in the stomach. There plainly existed an entire confusion in their ideas, to judge by all the disquiet and humming in and out of those that had recently come and possibly began to suspect something wrong and took a turn or two up and down in the room first, before the temptation became too great for them, and by the earlier arrivals that slowly crept up and down on the wall with acquired experience in life, or were lying stupefied and floundering on the window-sill.

"Ish!—and straight up into the washing water."

She looked with a certain indignation at the cause — her violet soap.

At the same time it opened a new train of thought while she smelled it two or three times.

"Mother's yellow soap is more honest."

She quickly threw it out of the window, and with

CHAPTER VI

a towel carefully wiped those that had fallen on the field of battle off the sill.

Later in the forenoon, Ma and Inger-Johanna stood down in the garden, picking sugar peas for dinner.

"Only the ripest, Inger-Johanna, which are becoming too hard and woody, till your father comes home. What will your aunt say when she hears that we have let you go with your father so far up in the wilderness — she certainly will not think such a trip very inviting, or comprehend that you can be so eloquent over stone and rocks."

"No, she thinks that nothing can compete with their Tulleröd," said Inger-Johanna, smiling.

"Pass the plate over to me, so that I may empty it into the basket," came from Ma.

"So aunt writes that Rönnow is going to stay all winter in Paris."

"Rönnow, yes — but I shall amuse myself very well by reading aloud to her this winter *Gedecke's Travels in Switzerland*, — and then give her small doses of my trip."

"Now you are talking without thinking, Inger-Johanna. There is always a great difference between that which is within the circle of culture and desolate wild tracts up here in the mountain region."

Ma's bonnet-covered head bowed down behind the pea-vines.

"Father says that it is surely because they want

to use him at Stockholm that he is going to perfect himself in French."

"Yes, he is certainly going to become something great. You can believe we find it ever so snug and pleasant when we are sometimes at home alone and I read aloud to aunt."

Ma's large bonnet, spotted with blue, rose up, and with a table knife in her hand she passed the empty plate back. "And he has the bearing which suits, the higher he gets."

"Quite perfect—but I don't know how it is, one does not care to think about him up here in the country."

Ma stood a moment with the table knife in her hand.

"That will do," she said, as she took up the basket, somewhat troubled—"We shan't have many peas this year," she added, sighing.

Chapter VII

THE kitchen at Gilje was completely given over to Christmas preparations.

There was a cold draught from the porch, an odor in the air of mace, ginger, and cloves—a roar of chopping-knives, and dull rumbling and beating so that the floor shook from the wooden mortar, where Great-Ola himself was stationed with a white apron and a napkin around his head.

At the head of the long kitchen table Ma was sitting, with a darning-needle and linen thread, sewing collared beef, while some of the crofter women and Thea, white as angels, were scraping meat for the fine meat-balls.

There, on the kitchen bench, with bloody, murderous arms, sat Thinka, who had recently returned home, stuffing sausages over a large trough. It went with great skill through the filler, and she fastened up the ends with wooden skewers, and struggled with one dark, disagreeable, gigantic leech after another, while their brothers or sisters were boiling in the mighty kettle, around which the flames crackled and floated off in the open fireplace.

The captain had come into the kitchen, and stood surveying the field of battle with a sort of pleasure. There were many kinds of agreeable prospects here for the thoughts to dwell upon, and samples of the finished products were continually being sent up to the office for him to give his opinion on.

"I'll show you how you should chop, girls," he said sportively, and took the knives from Torbjörg.

The two chopping-knives in his hands went up and down in the chopping-tray so furiously that they could hardly be distinguished, and awakened unmistakable admiration in the whole kitchen, while all paused in bewilderment at the masterpiece.

It is true, it continued for only two or three minutes, while Torbjörg and Aslak must stand with linen towels on their heads and chop all day.

But victory is still victory, and when the captain afterwards went into the sitting-room, humming contentedly, it was not without a little amused recollection of his strategy,—for, "yes, upon my soul," he could feel that his arms ached afterwards, nevertheless. And he rubbed them two or three times before he tied a napkin around his neck and seated himself at the table in order to do justice to the warm blood-pudding, with raisins and butter on it, which Thinka brought in to him.

"A little mustard, Thinka."

Thinka's quiet figure glided to the corner cupboard after the desired article.

"The plate might have been warmer for this kind of thing—it really ought to be almost burning hot for the raisins and butter."

CHAPTER VII

The always handy Thinka was out by the chimney in a moment with a plate. She came in again with it in a napkin; it could not be held in any other way.

"Just pour it all over on to this plate, father, and then you will see."

One of the happy domestic traits which Thinka had disclosed since her return home was a wonderful knack of managing her father; there was hardly any trace of peevishness any longer.

Thinka's quiet, agreeable pliancy and cool, even poise spread comfort in the house. The captain knew that he only needed to put her on the track of some good idea or other in the way of food, and something always came of it. She was so handy, while, when Ma yielded, it was always done so clumsily and with difficulty, just as if she creaked on being moved, so to speak, that he became fretful, and began to dispute in spite of it, notwithstanding she knew very well he could not bear it.

A very great deal had been done since Monday morning, and to-morrow evening it was to be hoped they would be ready. Two cows, a heifer, and a hog, that was no little slaughtering — besides the sheep carcasses.

"The sheriff—the sheriff's horse is in the yard," was suddenly reported in the twilight into the bustle of the kitchen.

The sheriff! It was lightning that struck.

"Hurry up to the office and get your father down to receive him, Jörgen," said Ma, composing herself. "You will have to take off the towels and then stop pounding, Great-Ola, exasperating as it is."

"They smell it when the pudding smokes in the kettle, I think," exclaimed Marit, in her lively mountain dialect. "Isn't it the second year he has come here just at the time of the Christmas slaughtering? So they are rid of the menfolk lying in the way at home among themselves."

"Your tongue wags, Marit," said Ma, reprovingly. "The sheriff certainly does not find it any too pleasant at home since he lost his wife, poor man."

But it was dreadfully unfortunate that he came just now — excessively unfortunate. She must keep her ground; it wouldn't do to stop things out here now. The captain came hastily out into the kitchen. "The sheriff will stay here till to-morrow — it can't be helped, Ma. I will take care of him, if we only get a little something to eat."

"Yes, that is easy to say, Jäger — just as all of us have our hands full."

"Some minced meat — fried meat-balls — a little blood-pudding. That is easy enough. I told him that he would have slaughter-time fare — and then, Thinka," he nodded to her, "a little toddy as soon as possible."

CHAPTER VII

Thinka had already started; she only stopped a moment at her bureau upstairs.

She was naturally so unassuming, and was not accustomed to feel embarrassed. Therefore she brought in the toddy tray like the wind, stopping only to put a clean blue apron on; and, after having spoken to the sheriff, went to the cupboard after rum and arrack, and to the tobacco table after some lighters, which she put down by the tray for the gentlemen before she vanished out through the kitchen door again.

"You must wash your hands, Torbjörg, and put things to rights in the guest-chamber; and then we must send a messenger for Anne Vaelta to help us, little as she is fit for. Jörgen, hurry!" came from Ma, who saw herself more and more deprived of her most needed forces.

Great-Ola had put up the sheriff's horse, and now stood pounding again at the mortar in his white surplice—thump, thump, thump, thump.

"Are you out of your senses out here? Don't you think?" said the captain, bouncing in; he spoke in a low voice, but for that reason the more passionately. "Are n't you going to mangle, too? Then the sheriff would get a thundering with a vengeance, both over his head and under his feet. It shakes the floor."

A look of despair came over Ma's face; in the sudden, dark, wild glance of her eye there almost shone rebellion—now he was beginning to drive her too far—But it ended in a resigned, "You can take the mortar with you out on the stone floor of the porch, Great-Ola."

And Thinka had to attend to the work of putting things in order and carrying in the supper, so that it was only necessary for Ma to sit there a little while, as they were eating, though she was on pins and needles, it is true; but she must act as if there was nothing the matter.

When Ma came in, there was a little formal talk in the beginning between her and the sheriff about the heavy loss he had suffered. She had not met him since he lost his wife, three months ago. It was lonesome for him now that he had only his sister, Miss Gülcke, with him. Both Viggo and Baldrian, which was a short name for Baltazar, were at the Latin school, and would not come home again till next year, when Viggo would enter the university.

The sheriff winked a little, and made a mournful gesture as if he wanted to convey an idea of sadly wiping one eyelash, but no more. He had given an exhibition of grief within nearly every threshold in the district by this time, and here he was in the house of people of too much common sense not to excuse him from any more protracted outburst just before a spread table with hot plates.

It developed into a rather long session at the table—with ever stronger compliments, as often

CHAPTER VII

as there was opportunity during the meal-time to catch a glimpse of the hostess, for every new dish that Thinka brought in smoking deliciously straight from the pan — actually a slaughtering feast — with a fine bottle of old ale in addition — for the new Christmas brew was too fresh as yet — and two or three good drams brought in just at the right time.

The sheriff also understood very well what was going on in the house, and how the hostess and Thinka were managing it.

The grown-up daughter cleared off the table and took care of everything so handily and comfortably without any bother and fuss — and so considerately. They had their pipes and a glass of toddy by their side again there on the sofa, with a fresh steaming pitcher, before they were aware of it.

The small inquisitive eyes of Sheriff Gülcke stood far apart; they looked into two corners at once, while his round, bald head shone on the one he talked to. He sat looking at the blond, rather slender young lady, with the delicate, light complexion, who busied herself so silently and gracefully.

"You are a fortunate man, you are, Captain," he said, speaking into the air.

"Have a little taste, Sheriff," said the captain consolingly, and they touched glasses.

"Nay, you who have a house full of comfort can talk — cushions about you in every corner —

so you can export to the city—But I, you see," —his eyes became moist—"sit there in my office over the records. I was very much coddled, you know—oh, well, don't let us talk about it. I must have my punishment for one thing and another, I suppose, as well as others.

"Isn't it true, Miss Kathinka," he asked when she came in, "it is a bad sheriff who wholly unbidden falls straight down upon you in slaughtering-time? But you must lend him a little home comfort, since it is all over with such things at his own home.

"Bless me, I had almost forgotten it," he exclaimed eagerly, and hastened, with his pipe in his mouth, to his document case, which hung on a chair near the door. "I have the second volume of *The Last of the Mohicans* for you from Bine Scharfenberg, and was to get—nay, what was it? It is on a memorandum—*A Capricious Woman*, by Emilie Carlén."

He took it out eagerly and handed it over to her, not without a certain gallantry.

"Now you must not forget to give it to me tomorrow morning, Miss Kathinka," he said threateningly, "or else you will make me very unhappy down at Bine Scharfenberg's. It won't do to offend her, you know."

Even while the sheriff was speaking, Thinka's eye glided eagerly over the first lines—only to make sure about the continuation—and in a twinkling she was down again from her room with the read-through book by Carlén and the first volume of the Mohicans done up in paper and tied with a bit of thread.

"You are as prompt as a man of business, Miss Thinka," he said jokingly, as with a sort of slow carefulness he put the package into his case; his two small eyes shone tenderly upon her.

Notwithstanding there had been slaughtering and hubbub ever since early in the morning, Thinka must still, after she had gone to bed, allow herself to peep a little in the entertaining book.

It was one chapter, and one more, and still one more, with ever weakening determination to end with the next.

Still at two o'clock in the morning she lay with her candlestick behind her on the pillow, and steadily read *The Last of the Mohicans*, with all the vicissitudes of the pursuits and dangers of the noble Uncas.

Ma wondered, it is true, that so many of the slender tallow candles were needed this winter.

The sheriff must have a little warm breakfast before going away in the morning.

And now he took leave, and thanked them for the hours that had been so agreeable and cheering, although he came so inconveniently—oh, madame, he knew he came at an inconvenient time. "Although now you have certainly got a right hand in household matters. Yes, Miss Thinka, I have tested you; one does not have the eye of a policeman for nothing.

"Invisible, and yet always at hand, like a quiet spirit in the house—is not that the best that can be said of a woman?" he asked, complimenting her fervently, when he had got his scarf around his fur coat, and went down to the sleigh with beaming eyes and a little grayish stubble of beard—for he had not shaved himself to-day.

"Pleasant man, the sheriff. His heart is in the right place," said the captain when, enlivened and rubbing his hands from the cold, he came in again into the sitting-room.

But father became ill after all the rich food at the slaughtering-time.

The army doctor advised him to drink water and exercise a good deal; a toddy spree now and then would not do him any harm.

And it did not improve the rush of blood to his head that Christmas came so soon after.

Father was depressed, but was reluctant to be bled, except the customary twice a year, in the spring and autumn.

After the little party for Buchholtz, the judge's chief clerk, on Thursday, he was much worse. He went about unhappy, and saw loss and neglect and erroneous reckonings in all quarters.

CHAPTER VII

There was no help for it, a messenger must go now after the parish clerk, Öjseth.

Besides his clerical duties, he taught the youth, vaccinated, and let blood.

What he was good for in the first named direction shall be left unsaid; but in the last it could safely be said that he had very much, nay, barrels, of the blood of the district on his conscience, and not least that of the full-blooded captain, whom he had bled regularly now for a series of years.

The effect was magnificent. After the sultry and oppressive stormy and pessimistic mood, which filled, so to speak, every groove in the house and oppressed all faces, even down to Pasop—a brilliant fair weather, jokes with Thinka, and wild plans that the family should go down in the summer and see the manoeuvres.

It was at the point of complete good humor that Ma resolutely seized the opportunity to speak about Jörgen's going to school—all that Aunt Alette had offered of board and lodging, and what she thought could be managed otherwise.

There was a reckoning and studying, with demonstration and counter-demonstration, down to the finest details of the cost of existence in the city.

The captain represented the items of expenditure and the debit side in the form of indignant questions and conjectures for every single one, as to whether she wanted to ruin him, and Ma stubbornly and persistently defended the credit side, while she went over and went over again all the items to be deducted.

When, time after time, things whirled round and round in the continual repetition, so that she got confused, there were bad hours before she succeeded in righting herself in the storm.

The captain must be accustomed to it slowly, until it penetrated so far into him that he began to see and think. But, like a persistent, untiring cruiser, she always had the goal before her eyes and drew near to it imperceptibly.

"This ready money"—it was for Ma to touch a sore, which nevertheless must be opened. The result was that the captain allowed himself to be convinced, and now became himself the most zealous for the plan.

Jörgen was examined in all directions. He was obliged to sit in the office, and the captain subjected him to the cramming process.

. . . .

"That's as old as the hills," read the captain. "If you swing a hen round and put her down backwards with a chalk mark in front of her beak, she will lie perfectly still; will not dare to move. She certainly believes it is a string that holds her. I have tried it ever so many times—that you may safely tell her, Thinka."

CHAPTER VII

"But why does Inger-Johanna write that?" asked Ma, rather seriously.

"Oh, oh,—for nothing—only so—"

Thinka had yesterday received her own letter, enclosed in that to her parents; it was a letter in regard to Ma's approaching birthday, which was under discussion between the sisters. And Inger-Johanna had given her a lecture in it, something almost inciting her to rebellion and to stick to her flame there in the west, if there really was any fire in it. That about the hen and the chalk mark was something at second-hand from Grip. Women could be made to believe everything possible, and gladly suffered death when they got such a chalk mark before their beaks!

That might be true enough, Thinka thought. But now, when all were so against it, and she saw how it would distress her father and mother, then — she sighed and had a lump in her throat — the chalk mark was really thicker than she could manage, nevertheless.

Inger-Johanna's letter had made her very heavy hearted. She felt so unhappy that she could have cried, if any one only looked at her; and as Ma did that several times during the day, she probably went about a little red-eyed.

At night she read *Arwed Gyllenstjerna*, by Van der Velde, so that the bitter tears flowed.

Her sister's letter also contained something on

her own account, which was not meant for her father and mother.

For you see, Thinka, when you have gone through balls here as I have, you do not any longer skip about blindly with all the lights in your eyes. You know a little by yourself; one way or another, there ought to be something in the manner of the person. Oh, this ball chat! I say, as Grip does: I am tired, tired, tired of it. Aunt is n't any longer so eager that I shall be there, though many times more eager than I.

There I am now looked upon as haughty and critical and whatever else it is, only because I will not continually find something to talk away about! Aunt now thinks that I have got a certain coldness of my own in my "too lively nature," a reserved calm, which is imposing and piquant—that is what she wants, I suppose! In all probability just like the ice in the steaming hot pudding among the Chinese, which we read about, you remember, in the *Bee*.

Aunt has so many whims this winter. Now we two must talk nothing but French together! But that she should write to Captain Rönnow that I was so perfect in it, I did not like at all; I have no desire to figure as a school-girl before him when he returns; neither is my pronunciation so "sweet," as she says!

I really don't understand her any longer. If there

was any one who could and ought to defend Grip at this time, it should be she; but instead of that, she attacks him whenever she can.

He has begun to keep a free Sunday-school or lecture for those who choose to come, in a hall out on Storgaden. It is something, you know, which creates a sensation. And aunt shrugs her shoulders, and looks forward to the time when he will vanish out of good society, although she has always been the first to interest herself in him and to say that he came with something new. It is extremely mean of her, I think.

Chapter VIII

JÖRGEN must start on his journey before the sleighing disappeared, for the bad roads when the frost was coming out might last till St. John's Day, and to harness the horses in such going would be stark madness. If he were not to lose a whole year, he must go early and be prepared privately for admission to school.

Jörgen was lost in meditations and thoughts about all that from which he was about to be separated. The gun, the sleds, the skis, the turning-lathe, the tools, the wind-mill, and the corn-mill left behind there on the hills, all must be devised with discretion — naturally to Thea first and foremost, on condition that she should take care of them till he came home again.

If he had been asked what he would rather be, he would doubtless have answered "turner," "miller," or "smith;" the last thing in the world which would have presented itself to his range of ideas, to say nothing of coming up as a bent or a longing, would have been the lifting up to the loftier regions of books. But Greece and Latium were lying like an unalterable fate across his path, so that there was nothing to do or even to think about.

On the day of his departure, the pockets of his new clothes, which were made out of the captain's

CHAPTER VIII

old ones, were a complete depository for secret despatches.

First, a long letter of fourteen pages, written in the night, blotted with tears, from Thinka to Inger-Johanna, in which with full details she gave the origin, continuation, and hopeless development of her love for Aas. She had three keepsakes from him—a little breastpin, the cologne bottle which he had given her on the Christmas tree, and then his letter to her with a lock of his hair on the morning he had to leave the office. And even if she could not now act against the wishes of her parents, but would rather make herself unhappy, still she had promised herself faithfully never to forget him, to think of him till the last hour.

The second despatch was from Ma to Aunt Alette, and contained—besides some economical propositions—a little suggestion about sounding Inger-Johanna when Captain Rönnow returned from Paris. Ma could not quite understand her this last time.

The captain had never imagined that there would be such a vacuum after Jörgen was gone. In his way he had been the occasion of so much mental excitement, so many exertions and anxieties, and so much heightened furious circulation of blood, that now he was away the captain had lost quite a stimulating influence. He had now no longer any one to look after and supervise with eyes in the back of his head, to exercise his acuteness on, or take by surprise—only the quiet, unassailable Thea to keep school with.

The doctor prescribed a blood-purifying dandelion tonic for him.

And now when the spring came—dazzling light, gleaming water everywhere, with melting patches of snow and its vanguards of red stone broken on the steep mountain sides—Thinka, with a case-knife in her numb hands, was out in the meadow gathering dandelion roots. They were small, young, and still tender, but they were becoming stronger day by day.

The captain, with military punctuality, at seven o'clock every morning emptied the cup prepared for him and stormed out.

To-day a fierce, boisterous, icy cold blast of rain with hail and snow met him at the outer door and blew far in on the floor. The sides of the mountains were white again.

These last mornings he was accustomed to run down over the newly broken-up potato field, which was being ploughed; but in this weather—

"We must give up the field work, Ola," he announced as his resolution in the yard—"it looks as if the nags would rather have to go out with the snow-plough."

He trudged away; it was not weather to stand

CHAPTER VIII

still in. The rain drove and pounded in showers down over the windows in the sitting-room with great ponds of water, so that it must be continually mopped up and cloths placed on the window-seats.

Ma and Thinka stood there in the gray daylight over the fruit of their common work at the loom this winter — a roller with still unbleached linen, which they measured out into tablecloths and napkins.

The door opened wide, and the captain's stout form appeared, enveloped in a dripping overcoat.

"I met a stranger down here with something for you, Thinka — wrapped up in oil-cloth. Can you guess whom it is from?"

Thinka dropped the linen, and blushing red advanced a step towards him, but immediately shook her head.

"Rejerstad, that execution-horse, had it with him on his trip up. He was to leave it here." The captain stood inspecting the package. "The sheriff's seal — Bring me the scissors."

In his officiousness, he did not give himself time to take his coat off.

"A para-sol! — A beautiful — new —" Thinka burst out. She remained standing and gazing at it.

"See the old — Hanged if the sheriff is n't making up to you, Thinka."

"Don't you see that here is 'philopena' on the seal, Jäger?" Ma put in, to afford a cover.

"I won a philopena from him——on New Year's Day, when father and I took dinner at Pastor Horn's—after church. I had entirely forgotten it," she said in a husky tone. Her eyes glanced from the floor halfway up to her parents, as she quietly went out, leaving the parasol lying on the table.

"I guess you will use your linen for a wedding outfit, Ma," said the captain, slapping his hands and swinging his hat with a flourish. "What would you say to the sheriff for a son-in-law here at Gilje?"

"You saw that Thinka went out, Jäger." Ma's voice trembled a little. "Very likely she is thinking that it is not long since his wife was laid in the grave. Thinka is very good, and would like to submit to us; but there may be limits to what we can ask." There was something precipitate in her movements over the linen, which indicated internal disturbance.

"The sheriff, Ma; is not he a catch? Fine, handsome man in his best years. Faith, I don't know what you women will have. And, Gitta," he reminded her, a little moved, "it is just the men who have lived most happily in their first marriage who marry again the soonest."

Time flew with tearing haste towards St. John's Day. Spring was brewing in the air and over the lakes. The meadow stood moist and damp, hillock on hillock, like the luxuriant forelocks of horses. The swollen brooks sighed and roared with freshly

CHAPTER VIII

shining banks. They boiled over, as it were, with the power of the same generating life and sap that made the buds burst in alder, willow, and birch almost audibly, and shows its nature in the bouncing, vigorous movements of the mountain boy, in his rapid speech, his lively, shining eyes, and his elastic walk.

At the beginning of summer a letter came from Inger-Johanna, the contents of which set the captain's thoughts into a new flight:

June 14, 1843

DEAR PARENTS,—At last a little breath to write to you. Captain Rönnow went away yesterday, and I have as yet hardly recovered my balance from the two or three weeks of uninterrupted sociability while he was here.

It will be pleasant to get out to Tilderöd next week on top of all this. It is beginning to be hot and oppressive here in the city.

There did not pass a day that we were not at a party, either at dinner or in the evening; but the pearl of them was aunt's own little dinners, which she has a reputation for, and at which we spoke only French. The conversation ran on so easily, one expresses one's self so differently, and our thoughts capture each other's already half guessed. Rönnow certainly speaks French brilliantly.

A man who carries himself as he does makes a

certain noble, masterly impression; you are transported into an atmosphere of chivalric manly dignity, and hear the spurs jingle, I had almost said musically; you almost forget that there are those who stamp their feet.

When I compare the awkward compliments at balls, which may come smack in your face, with Captain Rönnow's manner of saying and not saying and yet getting a thing in, then I do not deny that I get the feeling of a kind of exhilarating pleasure. He claimed that he had such an illusion from sitting opposite me at the table. I resembled so much a portrait of a historic lady which he had seen at the Louvre; naturally she had black hair and carried her neck haughtily and looked before her, smiling, with an expression which might have been characterized, "I wait—and reject—till he comes, who can put me in my right place."

Well, if it amuses him to think of such things, then I am happy to receive the compliments. It is true there are such godfathers and uncles who are utterly infatuated with their goddaughters, and spoil them with nonsense and sweets. I am afraid that Rönnow is a little inclined to this so far as I am concerned, for, sensible and straightforward as he always is, he continually launches out into superlatives in relation to me; and I really cannot help thinking that it is both flattering and pleasant when he is continually saying that I am made for pre-

CHAPTER VIII

this time from his trip to Paris with the full intent of completing his courting, after, like a wise and prudent general, having first surveyed the ground with his own eyes. Simply the manner in which he always addressed and paid his respects to her would have convinced a blind person of that.

The only one, however, who does not understand it, notwithstanding she is besieged in a thousand ways, is the object of his attentions herself. She sits there in the midst of the incense, truly protected against the shrewdness of the whole world by her natural innocence, which is doubly surprising, and, old Aunt Alette says, to be admired in her who is so remarkably clever.

I will not, indeed, absolve her from being a little giddy at all the incense which he and your sister-in-law incessantly burn before her (and what elderly, experienced person would not tolerate and forgive this in a young girl!) But the giddiness does not tend to the desired result, namely, the falling in love, but only makes her a little puffed up in her feeling of being a perfect lady, and is limited to her doing homage to him as the knightly cavalier and—her father's highly honored friend.

It is this, which he, so to speak, is for the present beaten back by, so he is going abroad again, and this evidently after consultation with your sister-in-law. Inger-Johanna, if my old eyes do not deceive me,—and something we two have seen and experienced, both separately and together, in this world, dear Gitta,—is not found ready for the matrimonial question, inasmuch as her vanity and pride have hitherto appeared as a feeling entirely isolated from this.

There was a snore from the leather-covered chair, and Ma continued, more softly:

She may, indeed, and that tolerably earnestly, wish to rule over a fine salon; but she has not yet been brought clearly to comprehend that with it she must take the man who owns it. There is something in her open nature which always keeps the distance between these two questions too wide for even a captain of cavalry to leap over it. God bless her!

Love is like an awakening, without which we neither know nor understand anything of its holy language; and unhappy are they who learn to know it too late, when they have imprisoned themselves in the so-called bonds of duty. I am almost absolutely sure that love has not yet been awakened in Inger-Johanna—may a good angel protect her!

"Ouf!—such old maids," said the captain, waking up. "Go on, go on—is there any more?"

How far the young student who has a position in

the office is in any degree a hindrance to these plans, I don't dare to say, either pro or con. But the governor's wife thinks or fears something, I am firmly convinced from her whole manner of treating him lately, although she is far too bright to let Inger-Johanna get even the slightest suspicion of her real reason.

I heard it plainly when I took coffee there on Sunday, before they went away to Tilderöd, and she had the maid tell him that she could not see him. There was a not very gracious allusion to his "Sunday professorship of pettifogging ideas," as she called it.

I suppose these must be something of the same sort of ideas that I was enthusiastic about when I was young and read Rousseau's *Émile*, which absorbed me very much, nay, which can yet occupy some of my thoughts. For she stated, as one of his leading ideas, that he, in his headlong blindness, thought that he could simplify the world, and first and foremost education, to a very few natural propositions or so-called principles. And you know, we ——still, that is going to be quite too long. To be brief, when Inger-Johanna with impetuosity rushed to the defence of Grip, she saw in him only the son of the idiotic "cadet at Lurleiken," as he is called, one of the well-known, amusing figures of the country; but this one, in addition to his father's distracted ideas, was also equipped with a faculty of using that fearful weapon, satire——*voilà* the phantom Grip!

Youthful student ideas could perhaps be used gracefully enough as piquant topics of conversation; but instead of that, to set them in motion in a headlong and sensational manner, without regard to the opinion of older people, was a great step, was pretentious, and showed something immature, something raw, which by no means ought to be relished.

I have reported this so much at length in order to show you by the very expressions that there may be here a "good deal of cotton in the linen," as the saying is.

And since I am going to bring my innermost heart to light, I shall have to tell you that he appears to me to be a trustworthy, truthful young man, whose natural disposition is as he speaks and not otherwise, and he carries a beautiful stamp on his countenance and in his whole bearing. If possibly he is a little forgetful of "My son, if you want to get on in the world, then bow," that is worst for him and not to his dishonor, we know.

It was also a truly refreshing enjoyment for me, as if looking into the kingdom of youth, awakening many thoughts, to talk with him, the two evenings this winter when he accompanied me, an old woman, home from the governor's (for him, I have no doubt, a very small pleasure), all the way out to the old

CHAPTER VIII

town, when otherwise I should have been obliged to go anxiously with my servant-girl and a lantern.

"Bah! nobody will attack her," growled the captain, bored.

Chapter IX

THE captain had had a genuine drive in the service ever since summer, when he and the lieutenant inspected the storehouse for the tents, together with the arsenal and the guns in the levying districts. Then the military exercises, and finally now the meeting of the commissioners of conscription. There had been tolerably lively goings-on at the inn in the principal parish the last two or three evenings with the army doctor, the solicitor Sebelow, tall Buchholtz, Dorff the sheriff's officer, and the lieutenants.

But the result was splendid in so far that, instead of the bay horse, he was now driving home with a fine three or four-year-old before the cariole, with a white star on the forehead and white stockings that almost promised to be a match for Svarten if—if—it were not a bolter.

It had just now, when the old beggar woman rose up from the ditch by the wayside, shown something in the eyes and ears which it certainly had concealed during all the three days of the session. He had at last even shot over its head to test it, without so much as the horse giving a start.

It would be too mean, after the doctor and First Lieutenant Dunsack had been unanimous in the same opinion as he about the beast, and he, besides,

CHAPTER IX

had given the horse-dealer twenty-five dollars to boot.

But now it trotted off with the cariole very steadily and finely. The little inclination to break into a canter was only unmannerliness and a little of coltish bad habits which stuck to it still, and would disappear by driving.

Great-Ola had not had a steadier horse in the stall by the side of Svarten, nevertheless—"You shall grow old in my barn; do you understand, you young Svarten? shall go to the city in pairs with your uncle—before the carriage for Inger—There now, you beast—of a—dog"—swip—swish—swip—swish—"I shall teach you to drop your bad habits, I shall. Whoa!" he thundered. "There! there!"

There was a whole train of gay fellows who were standing, talking, shouting, and drinking in the road outside the gate to the Bergset farm.

At the sight of the captain's well-known form they made way for him, greeting him politely. They knew that he had been far away, and the men who had gone to the mustering had just returned to the farms round about, yesterday and to-day.

"Fine, is n't he, Halvor Hejen? a lively colt—still, rather young."

"Maybe, captain. Fine, if he is n't skittish," replied the one spoken to.

"What is going on here — auction after Ole Bergset?"

"Yes; Bardon, the bailiff, is busy with the hammer in the room in there."

"So, so, Solfest Staale!" he said, winking to a young man, "do you believe there is anything in the story that Lars Överstadsbraekken is courting the widow here? Their lands lie very fine."

There came an ill-concealed amusement on the countenances of those standing about. They guessed what the captain was at. It was the rival he was speaking to.

"There is not any cow for sale that is going to calve in the fall, I suppose?"

There might be, they thought.

"Hold my horse a little while, Halvor, while I go and talk a little with the bailiff about it."

There was a crowd of people in the house, and the captain was greeted by one knot after another of noisy talking folk, men and women, girls and boys, among whom the brandy bottle was diligently circulating, until he got into the room where the sale was going on.

There sat Bardon in the crowded, steaming room, calling over and over again, with his well-known, strong, husky voice, threatening with the hammer, giving utterance to a joke, finally threatening for the last, last time, until with the law's blows he nailed the bid firmly forever down on the top

CHAPTER IX

of the table. They made way for the captain as he came.

"Are you also so crazy as to allow your wife to go to the auction, Martin Kvale?" he said, joking, to an important fellow with silver buttons on his coat, as he passed by.

Out in the hall stood the handsome Guro Granlien with a crowd of other young girls.

"Oh, Guro!" he said, chucking her under the chin, "now Bersvend Vaage has come home from the drill. He was in a brown study and wholly lost his wits, the fellow, and so I came near putting him in arrest: you are too hard on him, Guro." He nodded to the snickering girls.

Guro looked with great, staring eyes at the captain. How could he know that?

The captain knew the district in and out, forwards and backwards, as he expressed it. He had an inconceivably keen scent for contemplated farm trades, weddings, betrothals, and anything of the kind that concerned the young conscripts. Guro Granlien was not the first girl who opened her eyes wide on that account. He got a great deal out of his five subalterns, but by no means the least was to be found in his own always alert interest in these things.

And when, to-day, he made the little turn up to the place of auction, the reason was far less the "autumn cow," than his lively curiosity for the new things that might have happened during his long absence.

Therefore it was not at all unwelcome to him when the widow came out and invited him into the "other room," where he must at least have a drop of ale before he left the farm.

He was curious to get her on the confessional as to the possibility of a new marriage, and also had the satisfaction, after a half hour's confidential chat, of having won from her confidence the whole of the real and true condition of her thoughts about herself and the farm.

No one cheated him any longer about that affair, — the widow of Bergset was to retain undivided possession of the estate of the deceased and — not marry. But she was anxious not to let it come out; she wanted to be courted, of course — as a good match in the district, naturally.

The captain understood it very well: it was sly.

Something must also be said about something else at last, and so Randi, in the spirit of what had been said, added: "And the sheriff, who is going to marry again."

"So?"

"They say he is a constant visitor at the house of Scharfenberg, the solicitor. Very likely it is the youngest daughter, eh?"

"Don't know. Good-by, Randi."

He went quickly, so that his spurs rattled, and

his sabre flapped under his coat, down to his horse without looking to the right or left or speaking to any one. He pressed his shako more firmly down on his forehead before he got into the cariole.

"Thanks, Halvor. Give me the reins. There you—"

He gave young Svarten, who began with some capers, a taste of the whip, and off he went with tight reins at full trot, so that the fence-posts flew like drumsticks past his eyes.

In the quiet, hazy autumn day the cattle here and there were out on the highway.

A pig provoked him by obstinately running before the cariole.

"There, take care to get your stumps out of the way!"

It ended with a little cut on its back.

"See there! there is a beast of a cow lying in the middle of the road," he broke out, with his lips firmly pressed together.

"Well, if you won't get up, then you are welcome to stay! If you please—I am stupid also—I'll drive on."

His bitterness took full possession of him, and he would have firmly allowed the wheel to go over the animal's back if the latter had not risen up quickly at the last moment, so near that the captain's cariole was half raised up, while it grazed and was within an ace of being upset.

"Hm, hm," he mumbled, somewhat brought to his senses as he looked back upon the object of his missed revenge.

"So, so—off, I say, you black knacker—if you once peep back again in that way, I will kill you! Ha, ha, ha! If you run, you will still find a hill, my good friend."

He had had a tremendous headache all day; but it was not that which annoyed him—that he knew.

And when he came home, where they were expecting father to-day in great suspense after his long absence, his looks were dark.

"There, Ola! Curry the horse—dry him with a wisp of straw first—take good care of him—put a blanket on his back; do you hear? I only drove the fellow a little up the hill."

Great-Ola looked at the captain and nodded his head confidently, as he led the horse and carriage away from the steps; there was surely something the matter; the captain had got cheated again with this new nag.

"Good day, Ma—good day!" and he kissed her hastily. "Yes, I am quite well."

He took off his cloak and shako. "Oh, can't you let Marit take the trunk and the travelling-bag so that they need n't stand there on the steps any longer?—Oh, yes; it has been tiresome enough," as he evaded rather coldly Thinka's attentions.

CHAPTER IX

"Put the sabre on the peg, and carry the bag up to my chamber."

He himself went first up to the office to look at the mail, and then down to the stable to see how Great-Ola had treated Svarten.

There was something the matter with father; that was clear!

Ma's face, anxiously disturbed, followed him here and there in the doorways, and Thinka glided in and out without breaking the silence.

When he came in, the supper-table was spread —herring salad, decorated with red beets and slices of hard boiled eggs, and a glass of brandy by the side of it—and then half salted trout and a good bottle of beer.

Father was possibly not quite insensible, but extremely reticent. You could absolutely get only words of one syllable in answer to the most ingeniously conceived questions!

"The sheriff is going to marry again, they say; it is absolutely certain!" he let fall at last, as the first agreeable news he knew from the outer world; "Scharfenberg's youngest."

The remark was followed by deep silence, even if a gleam of perfect contentment glided over Thinka's face, and she busied herself with eating. They both felt that his ill-humor came from this.

"That man can say he is lucky with his daughters —Bine soon in a parsonage, and now Andrea the sheriff's wife! Perhaps you can get a position there, Thinka, when you need it some day, as governess for the children, or housekeeper; she won't be obliged to do more in the house than just what she pleases; she can afford it."

Thinka, blushing to the roots of her hair, kept her eyes on her plate.

"Yes, yes, Ma, as you make your bed you must lie in it in this world."

No more was said before Thinka cleared off the table, when Ma apologetically exclaimed, "Poor Thinka!"

The captain wheeled towards her on the floor with his fingers in the armholes of his vest and blinked indignantly at her.

"Do you know! After the parasol and the one attention after another which he has taken the pains to show all summer, if she could have given the man a bit of thanks and friendliness other than she has— It would not have gone so at all, if I had been at home!"— his voice rose to something like a peal of thunder—" But I think it is a flock of geese that I have here in the house, and not grown-up women who look out a little for themselves. Andrea Scharfenberg did n't let herself be asked twice, not she!" he said, walking out again when Thinka came in; he did not care if she did hear it.

Ma gazed somewhat thoughtfully at him, and in the

CHAPTER IX

days that followed, they petted and coddled father in every way to make him a little more cheerful. Thinka, in the midst of her quiet carefulness, cast her eyes down involuntarily, when he groaned and panted in this way.

He did not go out any farther than to look after young Svarten.

The horse had fever in one hoof to-day after the new shoeing. It was a nail which had been driven in too far by that blockhead of a smith. It must come out.

The captain stood silently looking on in his favorite position, with his arms on the lower half of the stable door, while Great-Ola, with the hind leg of young Svarten over his leg, was performing the operation of extraction with the tongs. The animal was good-natured and did not so much as move his leg.

"O–o–ola," came hoarsely, half smothered.

Great-Ola looked up.

"Good Lord!" if the captain did not sink slowly down, while he still held onto the stable door, right on the dung!

Ola looked a moment irresolutely at his master, dropping the horse's foot. Then he took the stable pail and spattered some water into his face until he once more manifested a little life and consciousness.

He then held the pail to his mouth.

"Drink, drink, Captain! Don't be afraid. It is only the result of all that drilling and pleasuring. It is just as it is when one has kept up a wedding festivity too long. My brother—"

"Help me out, Ola! There, let me lean on you—gently, gently. Ah, it does one good to breathe—breathe," as he stopped. "Now it's over, I believe. Yes, entirely over, nothing more than a half fainting spell. Just go with me a little bit, Ola, as a matter of precaution. Hm, hm, that goes well enough. Yes, yes, I have no doubt it is the irregular life the whole of the autumn. Go and call my wife. Say I am up in the chamber. I can manage the stairs bravely."

There was no little fright.

This time it was the captain who was at ease and turned it off, and Ma who without authority dispatched a messenger. If the army surgeon was not at home, then he must go to the district doctor.

When the army surgeon, Rist, came, and had received at the door Ma's anxious explanations that Jäger had had a slight shock, for the calming of the house he delivered a humorous lecture.

It was wholly a question of degree. The man who drank only so much that he stammered suffered from paralytic palsy of the tongue—and in this way every blessed man that he knew was a paralytic patient. This was only a congestion not uncommon among full-blooded people.

CHAPTER IX

Jäger himself was in fact so far over it that he demanded the toddy tray in the evening—true enough, only an extremely light dose for his part! But cock and bull stories from the encampment and about Svarten were told in the clouds of smoke, and with constant renewals of the thin essence, till half-past one in the morning.

There was a roaring in the stove on one of the following forenoons, while the captain sat in his office chair, and wrote so that his quill-pen sputtered.

As usual at this time of the year, after his long absence, there was a great multitude of things to be disposed of. Thea's Norwegian grammar was lying on the green table by the door; she had just finished reading, and was heard humming outside in the hall.

There was a noise on the stairs, and Ma showing some one the way up, "That way—to the captain."

There was a knocking at the door.

"Good day, my man! Well?"

It was an express from the sheriff—in Sunday dress—with a letter. It was to be given to the captain himself.

"What? Is there to be an answer? Well, well! Yes, go down to the kitchen and get a little something to eat and a dram.—Hm, hm," he mumbled and threw the letter, written on letter-paper and fastened with a seal, down on his desk, while in the mean time he took a turn up and down the floor. "Notice of the betrothal, I suppose—or perhaps an invitation to the wedding."

Opening it, he read it, standing up—eagerly running it over hastily—a cursed long introduction!—Over that—over that—quite to the third page.

"Well, there it comes!"

He struck the back of the hand in which he held the letter with a resounding whack into the other, and then seated himself—"Yes, yes, yes, yes, yes, yes, yes!"

He snapped his fingers, once, twice, three times, in a brown study, scratched his head behind his ear, and then slyly up under his wig.

"Now, we shall see—we shall see!—And that nonsense about Scharfenberg." He rushed to the door and jerked it open; but bethought himself and walked on tiptoe to the stairs. "Who is there in the hall—you, Thea?"

The little square-built, brown-eyed Thea flew up the stairs.

"Tell Ma to come up," he said, nodding.

Thea looked up at her father: there was something out of the ordinary about him.

When Ma came in, he walked about with the letter behind his back, clearing his throat. There

CHAPTER IX

was the suitable deliberate seriousness about him which the situation demanded.

"I have got a letter, Ma—from the sheriff!—Read!—or shall I read?"

He stood leaning against the desk, and went through its three pages, period by period, with great moderation, till he came to the point, then he hurled it out so that it buzzed in the air, and hugged Ma wildly.

"Well, well!—what do you say, Ma? Take a trip when we want to go down to our son-in-law!" He rubbed his hands. "It was a real surprise, Ma,—hm, hm," he began, again clearing his throat. "It is best that we ask Thinka to come up and tell her the contents—don't you think?"

"Ye–es," said Ma huskily, having turned to the door; she could see no help or escape for her any more, poor girl!

The captain walked up and down in the office, waiting. He had the high-spirited, dignified, paternal expression which is completely absorbed in the importance of the moment.

But where was she gone to?

She could not be found. They had hunted for her over the whole house.

But the captain was not impatient to-day.

"Well, then, don't you see her?" he mildly asked two or three times through the door.

At last Thea found her in the garret. She had

taken refuge up there and hid herself, when she saw the express and heard that it was from the sheriff, in anticipation of the contents. And now she was sitting with her head on her arms and her apron over her head.

She had not been crying; she had been seized with a sort of panic; she felt an irresistible impulse to hide herself away somewhere and shut her eyes, so that it would be really dark, and she would not be obliged to think.

She looked a little foolish when she went down with Thea to her father and mother in the office.

"Thinka," said the captain, when she came in, "we have received to-day from the sheriff an important letter for your future. I suppose it is superfluous to say—after all the attention you have allowed him to show you during the year—what it is about, and that your mother and I regard it as the greatest good fortune that could fall to your lot, and to ours also. Read the letter and consider it well. Sit down and read it, child."

Thinka read; but it did not seem as if she got far; she shook her head dumbly the whole time without knowing it.

"You understand very well, it is not any youthful love fancy, and any such exalted nonsense that he asks of you. It is if you will fill an honored position with him that you are asked, and if you

CHAPTER IX

can give the good will and care for him which he would naturally expect of a wife."

There was no answer to be got, except a weak groan down into her lap.

The captain's face began to grow solemn.

But Ma whispered, with a blaze of lightning in her eyes, "You see plainly, she cannot think, Jäger.—Don't you think as I do, father," she said aloud, "that it is best we let Thinka take the letter, so that she can consider it till to-morrow? It is such a surprise."

"Of course, if Thinka prefers it," came after them, from the captain, who was greatly offended, as Ma went with her, shutting her up in her chamber.

She had her cry out under the down quilt during the whole afternoon.

In the twilight Ma went up and sat beside her.

"No place to turn to, you see, when one will not be a poor, unprovided-for member of a family. Sew, sew your eyes out of your head, till at last you lie in a corner of some one's house. Such an honorable proposal would seem to many people to be a great thing."

"Aas! Aas, mother!" articulated Thinka very weakly.

"God knows, child, that if I saw any other way out, I would show it to you, even if I should have to hold my fingers in the fire in order to do it."

Thinka slipped her hand onto her mother's thin hand and sobbed gently into her pillow.

"Your father is no longer very strong—does not bear many mental excitements,—so that the outlook is dark enough. The attack when he came home last—"

When Ma went out, sigh followed sigh in the darkness.

Late in the evening Ma sat and held her daughter's head so that she could get some sleep; she was continually starting up.

And now when Thinka finally slept, without these sudden starts any longer—quietly and peacefully, with her fair young head regularly breathing on the pillow—Ma went out with the candle. The worst was over.

If the captain was in an exalted mood after having seen from the office window Aslak, who went as express messenger to the sheriff, vanishing through the gate, then in certain ways he was doubly set up in the kingdom of hope by a little fragment of a letter from Inger-Johanna, dated Tilderöd:

We are all in a bustle, packing up and moving to the city, therefore the letter will be short this time.

There have been guests here to the very last; solitude suits neither uncle nor aunt, and so they had said "Welcome to Tilderöd" so often that we had one long visit after another all through the summer—in perfect rusticity, it was said. But I believe indeed they did not go away again without feeling that aunt preserves style in it. With perfect freedom for every one, and collations both in the garden room and on the veranda, there is, after all, something about it which makes the guests feel that they must give something and be at their best. People don't easily sink down to the level of the commonplace when aunt is present. She flatters me that we are alike in that respect.

And I don't know how it is, I feel now that I am almost as much attracted by assemblies as formerly by balls. There certainly is much more of an opportunity to use whatever little wit one has, and they may be a real influential circle of usefulness: aunt has opened my eyes to that this summer. When we read of the brilliant French *salons*, where woman was the soul, we get an impression that here is an entire province for her. And to be able to live and work in the world has possessed me since I was little, and mourned so that I was not a boy who could come to be something.

I had got so far, dear parents, when Miss Jörgensen called me to go down into the garden to aunt. The mail had come from the office in the city, and on the table in a package lay a flat, red morocco leather box and a letter to me.

It was a gold band to wear in my hair, with a

yellow topaz in it, and in the letter there was only, "To complete the portrait. RÖNNOW."

Of course aunt must try it on me at once — take down my hair, and call in uncle. Rönnow's taste was subtly inspired when it concerned me, she declared.

Oh, yes! it is becoming.

But with the letter and all the fantastical overvaluation, there is that which makes me feel that the gold band pinches my neck. Gratitude is a tiresome virtue.

Aunt lays so many plans for our social life next winter, and is rejoicing that Rönnow may possibly come for another trip.

For my part I must say I don't really know; I both want it and don't want it.

Chapter X

THE more quickly and quietly the wedding could be arranged, the better, said the sheriff. It had its advantage in getting ahead of explanations and gossip. People submitted to an accomplished fact.

The third day of Christmas was just the right one to escape too much sensation; and it suited the sheriff exactly, so that he could enter upon his new state of household affairs with the new year.

Naturally, Kathinka was asked about every one of these points; and she always found everything that her father thought right.

The decision that the wedding should be arranged speedily and promptly was exactly after the captain's own heart. On the other point, on the contrary, that everything should be kept so quiet and still, he was in agreement with the sheriff and Ma, of course; but it really did not lie in his nature that the whole joyful affair should take place smothered with a towel before his mouth, and whispering on tiptoe, as if it were a sick-room they were having at Gilje instead of a wedding.

Some show there must be about it; that he owed to Thinka, and to himself also a little.

And thus it came about that before Christmas he took a little sleighing trip, when it was good going, down to the lieutenant's and to the solicitors,

Scharfenberg and Sebelow, with whom he had some money settlements to get adjusted in regard to the map business that had been done in the last two suits.

And then, when he met the report that the banns had been published in church for his daughter and the sheriff, he could answer with a question if they would not come and convince themselves. Confidentially, of course, he invited no one but the army surgeon and those absolutely necessary. "But"—winking—"old fellow, how welcome you shall be, the third day of Christmas, not the second and not the fourth, my boy, remember that!"

And he took care that provisions as well as batteries of strong liquors should be stored up inside the ramparts at home, so the fortress could hold its own.

On Christmas Eve there came a horse express from the sheriff with a sleigh full of packages—nothing but presents and surprises for Thinka.

First and foremost, his former wife's warm fur cloak with squirrel-skin lining and muff, which had been made over for Thinka by Miss Brun in the chief parish; then her gold watch and chain with earrings, and rings, all like new, and burnished up by the goldsmith in the city, and a Vienna shawl, and, lastly, lavender water and gloves in abundance.

In the letter he suggested to his devotedly loved Kathinka that his thoughts were only with her

CHAPTER X 187

until they should soon be united by a stronger bond, and that she, when once in her new home, would find several other things which might possibly please her, but which it would not be practical to send up to Gilje, only to bring them right back again.

He had not brought Baldrian and Viggo home for Christmas—and in this he hoped she would agree with him; he had sent them down to his brother, the minister at Holmestrand.

Never in Great-Ola's time had there been such a festive show in horses and vehicles, as when, on the third day of Christmas, they started down the hill to the annex-church; the harnesses and bells shone, and both the black horses glistened before the double sleighs, as if they had been polished up, both hair and mane.

Under the bearskin robe in the first sat the captain in a wolf-skin coat and Thinka adorned with the chains and clothes of the sheriff's first wife, with young Svarten. In the second Ma and Thea, with Great-Ola on the dickey seat behind and old Svarten.

There stood the subalterns in uniform paying their respects at the church door; and inside, in the pew, Lieutenants Dunsack, Frisak, Knebelsberger, and Knobelauch rose up in full uniform. So the sheriff could see that there was some style about it, anyway.

And when they turned towards home, after the ceremony was over, now with the captain and his wife in the first sleigh and the wedded couple in the other—there was such a long cortège that the sheriff's idea of celebrating the wedding quietly must be regarded as wholly overridden.

At Gilje dinner was waiting.

During this the powers of the battalion from the youngest lieutenant up to the captain developed a youthful courage in their attack on the strong wares, so wild and so regardless of the results, that it could only demand of the sheriff a certain degree of prudence.

All would drink with the bride and the bridegroom, again and again.

The sheriff sat contented and leaning forward with his great forehead thinly covered with hair, taking pains to choose his words in the cleverest and most fitting manner for the occasion.

And so long as it was confined to the speeches, he was the absolute master, unless he might possibly have a rival in the army surgeon's sometimes more deeply laid satire, which became more problematical and sarcastic after he had been drinking.

But now the small twinkling eyes, shining more and more dimly and tenderly veiled, devoted themselves exclusively to the bride.

She must taste the tower tart and the wine custard, for his sake! He would not drink any more,

CHAPTER X

if he could avoid it, for her sake. "I assure you," for your—only for your sake."

An inroad was made on the wares at Gilje with prolonged hilarity till far into the night, when some of the sleighs in the starlight and in the gleam of the Northern lights reeled homewards with their half unconscious burdens drawn by their sober horses, while as many as the house would hold remained over in order to celebrate the wedding and Christmas the next day.

By New Year's the house was finally emptied of its guests, the sheriff and Kathinka were installed in their home, and the captain travelled down on a visit to them with Thea in order to have his New Year's Day spree there.

But then Ma was tired out and completely exhausted.

She felt, now the wheel of work had stopped all at once, and she sat there at home alone, on the day after New Year's, how tremendous a load it had been to pull. The trousseau all through the autumn and the household affairs before the holidays, Christmas, and the wedding, and all the anxieties.

It had gone on incessantly now, as far back as she could think. It was like ravelling out the yarn from a stocking, the longer she thought, the longer it was, clear back to the time when it seemed to her there was a rest the days she was lying in childbed.

But that was now long since.

She was sitting in the corner of the sofa half asleep in the twilight, with her knitting untouched before her.

Aslak and two of the girls had got leave to go to a Christmas entertainment down at the Skreberg farm, and except old Torbjörg, who was sitting with her hymn book and humming and singing in the kitchen, there was no one at home.

Bells jingled out in the yard. Great-Ola had come home with the two-seated sleigh and old Svarten, after having driven the captain and Thea.

He stamped the snow off in the hall and peeped in through the door.

When he drove past Teigen, the postmaster had come out with the captain's mail.

"When did you get there last evening? I hope Thea was not cold."

"No, not at all! We were down there in good time before supper. Ever so many messages from the young wife; she was down in the stable and patted and stroked Svarten last night. It was kind of a separation."

Ma rose. "There is a candle laid out for the stable lantern."

Great-Ola vanished again.

Old Svarten, still harnessed to the sleigh, stood in the stable door and neighed impatiently.

"It only lacked that you should turn the key also," growled Ola, while he took off the harness,

CHAPTER X

and, now with the harness and bells over his arm, let the horse walk in before him.

"Why, if young Svarten is n't neighing also! That was the first time you have said a decent good day here in the stable, do you know that? But you will have to wait, you see."

He curried and brushed and rubbed the new arrival like a privileged old gentleman. They had been serving together now just exactly nine years.

In the kitchen the spruce wood crackled and snapped on the hearth, casting an uncertain reddish glow over Ma's newly polished copper and tin dishes and making them look like mystical shields and weapons hung on the walls.

Great-Ola was now sitting there making himself comfortable with his supper, Christmas cheer and entertainment — butter, bread, bacon, wort-cakes, and salt meat; and Torbjörg had been ordered to draw a bowl of small beer for him down in the cellar. Ola had heard one thing and another down there.

Thinka, she had gone out into the kitchen and would take charge of the housekeeping immediately. But there she found some one who meant to hold the reins.

Old Miss Gülcke would n't hear of that. She went straight up to the office, they said, and twisted and turned it over with her brother the whole forenoon till she got what she wanted.

And in the evening the sheriff sat on the sofa and talked so sweetly to the young wife. Beret, the chamber-maid, heard him say that he wanted her to have everything so extremely nice and be wholly devoted to him, so that—Horsch, the old gray-beard! We can see now what he was doing here last year.

"And thereby," said Ola, with a mouthful between his teeth, while he cut and spread a new slice of bread, "she got rid of the trouble and the management too."

"It is of no use to pull the noose when one has his head in a snare, you see, Ola."

In the sitting-room Ma had examined the mail that had come, sitting by the stove door. Besides a number of *Hermoder*, *The Constitutional*, and a free official document, there was a letter from Aunt Alette.

She lighted the candle and sat down to read it.

In certain respects it was a piece of good fortune that Jäger was not at home. He ought to have nothing to do with this.

DEAR GITTA,—I have taken the second Christmas day to write down for you my thoughts concerning Inger-Johanna. I cannot deny that she has come to interest me almost more than I could wish; but, if we can feel a certain degree of anxiety for the smallest flower in our window, which is just going

CHAPTER X

to blossom, how much more then for a human bud, which in the developing beauty of its youth is ready to burst out with its life's fate. This is more than a romance, it is the noble art work of the Guide of all, which in depth and splendor and immeasurable wealth surpasses everything that human fantasy is able to represent.

Yes, she interests me, dear Gitta! so that my old heart almost trembles at thinking of the life path which may await her, when rise or fall may depend on a single deceptive moment.

What can Nature mean in letting such a host of existences, in which hearts are beating, succumb and be lost in this choice, or does it thereby in its great crucible make an exact assay, without which nothing succeeds in passing over into a more complete development—who can unriddle Nature's runes? My hope for Inger-Johanna is that the fund or the weight of personality, which she possesses in her own nature, will preponderate in the scales of her choice in the decisive moment.

I premise all this as a sigh from my innermost heart; for I follow with increasing dread how the path is made more and more slippery under her feet, and how delicately your sister-in-law weaves the net around her, not with small means to which Inger-Johanna would be superior, but with more deep-lying, sounding allurements.

To open up the fascinating prospect of making

her personal qualities and gifts count—what greater attraction can be spread out before a nature so ardently aspiring as hers? It is told of Englishmen that they fish with a kind of counterfeited, glittering flies, which they drag over the surface of the water until the fish bites; and it appears to me that in no less skilful manner your sister-in-law continually tempts Inger-Johanna's illusions. She never mentions the name of the one concerned, so that it may dawn upon her of itself.

Only the careless hint to me, in her hearing, the last time I was there, that Rönnow had certainly for some time been rather fastidiously looking for a wife among the *élite* of our ladies—why was not that calculated to excite, what shall I call it, her ambition or her need of having a field of influence?

Perhaps I should not have noticed this remark to that extent if I had not seen the impression it made on her; she was very absent-minded and lost in thoughts.

And yet the question of whether one should give her heart away ought to be so simple and uncomplicated! Are you in love? Everything else only turns on—something else.

The unfortunate and fateful thing is if she imagines she is able to love, binds herself in duty to love, and thinks that she can say to her immature heart: You shall never awaken. Dear Gitta, sup-

CHAPTER X

pose it did awaken — afterwards — with her strong, vigorous nature?

It is that which hovers before me so that I have been compelled to write. To talk to her and make her prudent would be to show colors to the blind; she must believe blindly in the one who advises her. Therefore it is you, Gitta, who must take hold and write.

Ma laid the letter down in her lap; she sat in the light, looking paler and sharper even than common.

It was easy for Aunt Alette, the excellent Aunt Alette, to think so happily that everything should be as it ought to be. She had her little inheritance to live on and was not dependent on any one. But — Ma assumed a dry, repellent expression — without the four thousand, old and tormented in Miss Jörgensen's place at the governor's, she would not have written that kind of angelic letter.

Ma read on:

I must also advance here some further doubts, so that you will certainly think this is a sad Christmas letter. This, then, is about dear Jörgen, who finds it so hard at school. That he has thus far been able to keep up with his class, we owe to Student Grip, who, persistently and without being willing ever to hear a word about any compensation, has gone over with him and cleared up for him his worst stumbling-blocks, the German and the Latin grammar.

And if I now express his idea in regard to Jörgen, it is with no small degree of confidence that it may be well founded. He says that so far from Jörgen's having a poor head, it is just the opposite. Only he is not made for the abstract, which is the requisite for literary progress, but all the more for the practical.

In connection with a sound, clear judgment, he is both dexterous and inventive. Jörgen would be an excellent mechanic or even a mechanical engineer, and would come to distinguish himself just as certainly as he will reap trouble, difficulty, and only extremely moderate results by toiling from examination to examination in his studies.

To be sure, I cannot subscribe to Student Grip's somewhat youthful wild ideas about sending him to be an apprentice in England (or even so far as to the American Free States!) inasmuch as a mechanic cannot here obtain a respected rank in society, such as is said to be the case in the above named lands.

Still, much of this, it seems to me, is worth taking into serious consideration.

I sometimes almost doubt whether, old as I am, nevertheless I might be too young. Call it the fruit of inner development or simply an attraction, but the thoughts of the young always exert an enlivening and strengthening influence on my hope of life. Still, I never reconcile myself to the thought

CHAPTER X 197

that our ideals must inevitably, by a kind of natural law, become exhausted and weakened and break from age like any old earthenware.

And when I see a young man like Grip judged so severely by the so-called practical men—not, so far as I understand, for his ideas of education, but because he would sacrifice himself and put them in operation—I cannot avoid giving him my whole sympathy and respect.

Now he has abandoned law and devoted himself to the study of philology; for, he says, in this country no work is of any use without a sign-board, and he will now try to get a richly gilded one in an excellent examination, seize hold of untrodden soil, like the dwarf birches upon the mountain, and not let go, even if a whole avalanche comes over him.

When it is considered that he must work hard and teach several hours daily only to be able to exist, I cannot but admire his fiery courage and—true, I have not many with me—wish him good luck.

Ma sat pondering.

Then she cut out the page which spoke of Jörgen. It might be worth while, if opportunity offered, to show it to Jäger. In the simplicity of her heart, she really did not know what to think.

Chapter XI

EVERYTHING was white now in the very heart of winter, white from the window-panes in the sitting-room to the garden, the fields, and the mountain slopes, white as the eye glided over the mountain-tops up to the sky, which lay like a semi-transparent, thickly frosted window-pane and shut it all in.

It was cold here, the warm-blooded captain maintained. He began to amuse himself with feeling and tracing out where there was a draught, and then with pasting long strips of paper with cloth and oakum under it. And then he used to go out from his work, with only his wig, without his hat, and chat with the people in the stable or at the barn, where they were threshing.

They were lonely there now with only Ma, Thea, and himself; no one understood what Thinka had been for him!

At last he ended in pondering on laying out fox-traps and traps and spring-guns for wolves and lynx in the hill pastures.

Ma was obliged a hundred times a day to answer what she thought, even if she had just as much idea about it as about pulling down the moon.

"Yes, yes, do it, dear Jäger."

"Yes, but do you believe it will pay—that is what

CHAPTER XI

I am asking about—to go to the expense of fox-traps?"

"If you can catch any, then—"

"Yes, if—"

"A fox skin is certainly worth something."

"Had n't I better try to put out bait for lynx and wolf?"

"I should think that would be dearer."

"Yes, but the skin—if I get any; it depends on that, you see."

Then he would saunter thoughtfully out of the door, to come back an hour later and again and again fill her ears with the same thing.

Ma's instinct told her that the object of his first catch was really she; if she allowed herself to be fooled into giving positive advice, he would not forget to let her feel the responsibility for the result, if it should be a loss.

To-day he had again been pondering and going over the affair with her, when they were surprised by the sheriff's double sleigh driving up to the steps.

The hall door, creaking with the frost, flew open under the captain's eager hand.

"In with you into the sitting-room, Sheriff."

Behind his wolf-skin coat Thinka emerged, stately and wrapped up in furs.

"Your most obedient servant, kinsman, and friend."

The sheriff was on a business trip farther up, and asked for hospitality for Thinka for two or three days, till he came back; he would not omit to claim her again promptly. And, in the next place, he must ask of his father-in-law the loan of a small sleigh for his further journey; he should be way up in Nordal's annex this evening.

Thinka already had Torbjörg and Thea competing each for one of her snow-stockings to get them off, and Marit was not free from eagerly peeping in at the door.

"You shall, in any event, have a little something to eat and some tea-punch, while the horse gets its breath, and they make the sleigh ready."

The sheriff did not have much time to waste, but the sun of family life shone too mildly here for him not to give a half hour, exactly by the clock.

He made one or two attempts to get his things off, but then went to Thinka.

"You have tied the knot in my silk handkerchief so well that you will have to undo it yourself. Thanks, thanks, my dear Thinka.—She spoils me completely. Nay, you know her, Captain."

"You see what she has already begun to be for me," he said later, appealing with a pleasant smile to his father-in-law and mother-in-law at the hastily served collation—he must have his tea-punch poured out by Thinka's hand.

When the sheriff, carefully wrapped up by his

young wife, was followed out to the sleigh, Thinka's tea stood there almost untouched and cold; but Ma came now with a freshly filled hot cup, and they could sit down to enjoy the return home in peace.

He is certainly very good, Ma thought—he had guessed that Thinka was homesick.

"The sheriff is really very considerate of you, Thinka, to let you come home so soon," she said.

"Fine man! Would have to hunt a long time for his like!" exclaimed the captain with a full, strong bass. "Treats you like a doll, Thinka."

"He is as good as he can be. Next week Miss Brun is coming to make over a satin dress for me; it has only been worn once. Gülcke will have me so fine," said Thinka, by way of illustration. The tone was so quiet that it was not easy for Ma to tell what she meant.

"The fellow stands on his head for you; don't know what he will hit upon."

Besides his wish to meet his wife's longing for home, the sheriff may possibly also have determined to take her with him from a little regard for the younger powers in the principal parish—Buchholtz and Horn. They had begun to visit at his house somewhat often and evidently to feel at home there, after a young, engaging hostess had come to the house.

Towards evening the captain had a quiet game of picquet.

It seemed as if comfort accompanied Thinka. Her mediatorial and soothing nature had come to the house again; it was felt both in parlor and kitchen.

Father came again in the forenoon for a little portion of oat cake and whey cheese when they were cooking salt meat and peas in the kitchen, and Ma found first one thing and then another done for her and was anticipated in many handy trifles, notwithstanding that Thinka also had to finish a pair of embroidered slippers that Gülcke had expressed a wish for. But there was plenty of time for that. She got well along on the pattern while her father was taking his noonday nap, and she sat up there and read him to sleep.

The captain found it so comfortable when he saw the needle and worsted flying in Thinka's hand — it was so peacefully quiet — it was impossible not to go to sleep.

And then he was going to have her for only three days.

While her fingers were moving over the canvas, Kathinka sat having a solitary meditation —

Aas had sent her a letter when he heard of her marriage. He had believed in her so that he could have staked his life on her constancy, and even if many years were to have passed, he would have worked, scrimped, and scraped in order at last to have been able to reach her again, even if they should then both have left their youth behind them. It had been his joyful hope that she would keep firm and wait for him even through straits and poor circumstances. But now that she had sold herself for goods and gold, he did not believe in any one any more. He had only one heart, not two; but the misfortune was, he saw it more plainly, that she also had—

"Huf! I thought I heard you sighing deeply," said the captain, waking up; "that comes from lying and struggling on one's back. Now we shall have some coffee."

Even if Thinka could not answer Aas, still she would try to relieve her heart a little to Inger-Johanna. She had brought her last letter with her to answer in this period of calm at home, and was sitting up in her room with it before her, in the evening.

"Inger-Johanna is fortunate, as she has nothing else to think of," she said to herself, sighing and reading:

And you, Thinka, you also ought to have your eye on your part of the country, and make something out of the place into which you have now come; it is indeed needed up there, for there is no doubt that society has its great mission in the refinement of customs and the contest against the crude, as aunt expresses it.

I am not writing this for nothing, nor wholly

in the air; I stand, indeed, too near to many conditions to be able to avoid thinking of the possibility of sometime being placed in such a position. If I said anything else, I should not be sincere.

And I must tell you, I see a great many things I should like to help in. It must be that a place can be found for a good many ideas which now, as it were, are excommunicated.

Society ought to be tolerant, aunt says; why, then, cannot such views as Grip's be discussed peacefully? The first thing I would do would be to go in for being extravagant and defending them. In a woman, nevertheless, this is never anything more than piquancy. But ideas also must fight their way into good society.

I ponder and think more than you can imagine; I feel that I ought to put something right, you see.

And I am not any longer so struck with the wisdom of men altogether. A woman like aunt keeps silent and pulls the strings; but you can never imagine how many are led by her strings. She is, between ourselves, a little diplomatic, in an old-fashioned way, and full of flourishes, so that she almost makes it a pleasure to have it go unobserved and by a roundabout way. Straight out would many times be better, I believe; at any rate, that is my nature.

And still a little warning with it, Thinka (oh, how I feel I speak as if I were in aunt's skin!) Remem-

CHAPTER XI

ber that no one ever rules a room except from a place on the sofa; I know you are so modest that they are always getting you off on the chairs. You are not at all so stupid as you imagine; only you ought not to try to hide what you think.

If I should sometime meet Grip again, I should convince him that there may be other ways to Rome than just going head foremost at it! I have got a little notion of my own since he last domineered me, with his contempt for society, and was always so superior. But I have not had more than one or two glimpses of him on the street the whole winter. He is so taken up by his own affairs; and it is n't proper, uncle says, to invite him to *soirées*, since he has pledged himself to certain strong ideas, which one does not dare to hint at without provoking a very serious dispute. In one or two gentlemen parties he has been entirely too grandiloquent—drank too much, uncle thought. But I know so well why. He must hit upon something, he used to say, when he gets tired and bored too much, and at the Dürings there is a dreadful vacuum.

Thinka had read the letter through; there might be much to think of, but she was so taken up by Aas—she was never done with rolling that millstone.

. . . .

During the monotony of winter, in the middle of February, a letter was received, which the captain at first weighed in his hand and examined two or three times — white, glossy vellum paper, C. R. in the seal — and he tore it open.

Yes, to be sure, it was from Rönnow! — his brilliant, running hand with the peculiar swing, which brought him to mind, as his elegant form, with a jaunty tread, moved up and down.

CAPTAIN PETER JÄGER, — Highly esteemed, dear old comrade and friend:

I shall not preface this with any long preludes about position in life, prospects, etc., but go straight on with my prayer and request.

As you have seen that my cards are lucky — really more as they have been dealt than as I have played them — you will certainly understand that in the last two or three years I have found it proper to look about for a wife and a partner for life who would be suitable for my condition. But during the whole of my seeking there was hidden in the most secret corner of my heart a black-haired, dark-eyed girl, whom I first saw by the card-table one winter evening up at Gilje, and whom I have since seen again and again with ever more fascination during her development into the proud woman and lady whose superior nature was incontestable.

Now, with my round six-and-forty years, I shall

CHAPTER XI

not hold forth with any long tale of my love for her, although, perhaps, there might be a good deal to say on that point also. That I am not old inwardly I have at all events fully found out on this occasion.

It goes without saying that I do not address my prayer to you without having first satisfied myself by a close and long acquaintance that your daughter also could cherish some feelings responsive to mine.

That the result has not been to my disadvantage is apparent from her precious reply to me, received yesterday, in which I have her yes and consent.

In the hope that a sincere conduct and intention will not be misconstrued, I herewith address the prayer and the question to you and your dear wife —whether you will trust to me the future of your precious Inger-Johanna?

What a man can do to smooth and make easy her path of life, that I dare promise, on my *parole d'honneur*, she shall never lack.

I will also add that when the court, towards the end of May or the early part of June, goes to Christiania, I shall be on duty and go too. I shall then be able again to see her on whom all my hope and longing are placed.

In anxious expectation of your honored answer,
Most respectfully,
Your always faithful friend,
CARSTEN RÖNNOW

Here was something better to think about than to talk with Ma about fox-traps and spring-guns.

There would not be any after-dinner nap to-day.

He rushed out into the yard with great force: another man must thresh in the barn; the manure must be drawn out; they must hurry!

He came in and seated himself on the sofa and lighted a lamplighter, but jumped up again while he held it to his pipe. He remembered that a message must be sent to the smith to mend the harrows and tools for spring.

There was no help for it, he must go down and tell the news to the sheriff himself.

Chapter XII

DURING the first days of March Inger-Johanna wrote:

This comes so close upon my former, because I have just received a letter from Rönnow about something on which I would gladly, dear parents, have you stand on my side, when you, as I foresee, receive aunt's explicit and strong representation and reasons in the opposite direction.

Rönnow already writes as if it were something certain and settled that we should have the wedding in the summer, in June or July. Aunt wants it at her house, and hopes that, in any event, you, father, will come down.

Rönnow urges so many amiable considerations which speak for it, and I do not at all doubt that aunt in her abundant kindness will take care to make it doubly sure with a four-page letter full of reasons.

But against all this I have only one thing to say, that I, at the time I gave my consent to Rönnow, did not at all foresee such haste without, as it were, a little time and breathing-space for myself.

It is possible that others cannot understand this feeling of mine, and especially it seems that aunt thinks it does not exactly show the degree of heartiness of feeling that Rönnow could expect.

But to the last, which is certainly the only one of the whole number she can urge that is worth answering, I will only say, that it cannot possibly be Rönnow's intent to offend my innermost sensibilities when he learns how I feel about it.

I only ask for suitable time—for instance, till some time next winter. I should so much like to have this year, summer and autumn at least, a little in quiet and peace. There is so much to think over, among other things my future position. I want first to study the French grammar through, and I should prefer to do it at home alone, and generally to prepare myself. It is not merely like jumping into a new silk dress.

Oh, I wish, I wish, I wish I could be at Gilje this summer! I sat yesterday thinking how delightful it was there last year on the high mountains!

No, aunt and I would not agree permanently. Her innermost, innermost peculiarity (let it be never so well enveloped in amiability and gentle ways of speech) is that she is tyrannical. Therefore she wants now to manage my wedding, and therefore—which can now vex and disturb me, so that I haven't words for it!—she has in these days got my good-natured (but not especially strong-minded, it would be a pity to say that!) uncle to commit the act, which is far from being noble, of dismissing Grip from his position in the office. It is just like robbing him of half of what is needed to enable him

CHAPTER XII

to live and study here, and that only because she does not tolerate his ideas.

I let her know plainly what I thought about it, that it was both heartless and intolerant; I was so moved.

But why she pursues him to the seventh and last—for with aunt there is always something for the seventh and last—that I should still like to know.

Regard must naturally be paid to Inger-Johanna's wish to postpone the wedding. And so there was writing and writing to and fro.

But then came Rönnow's new promotion and with it the practical consideration, which weighed on the scales, that housekeeping must be begun on moving-day in October.

. . . .

There was a general brushing up at Gilje from top to bottom, inside and out. The rooms upstairs must be whitened and everything put in order for the arrival of the newly married couple to remain this summer, the whole of July, after the wedding.

And when Inger-Johanna should come she was to meet a surprise—the whole of the captain's residence, by order of the army department, newly painted red with red-lead and white window sashes.

The captain's every-day coat had a shower of

spots at all times in the day, as he stood out by the painter's ladder and watched the work — first the priming and now the second coat; then came the completion, the third and last. The spring winds blew, so that the walls dried almost immediately.

He was a little dizzy off and on during all this, so that he must stop and recover his balance; but there was good reason for it, because the parish clerk this year had not taken enough blood, since he had become so much stouter!—and then perhaps he pushed on too hard and eagerly; for he did long for Inger-Johanna's return.

He talked of nothing but Inger-Johanna, of her prospects, beauty, and talents, and how Ma could not deny that he had seen what there was in her from the time when she was very small.

But Ma still thought privately, while he was going about boisterous and happy, that he had been less stout and more healthy when he had more anxieties and had to take the world harder. She had let him into the secret of Aunt Alette's misgivings in respect to Jörgen's capacities for scholarship.

"I have not been able to avoid thinking, Jäger, that Jörgen might not find happiness in that line."

"In what line, then?—Be a shoemaker and lie on one knee and take the measure of us others, perhaps—Oh-ho, no," stretching himself with superabundant conviction, "if we can afford to keep him at his studies, he can easily learn. There are many

CHAPTER XII

more stupid than he who have attained the position of both minister and sheriff."

One day the captain hastily separated a letter from Aunt Alette from his official mail, and threw it on the table for Ma to read through at her convenience. If there was anything in it, she could tell it to him, he shouted back, as he went up the stairs to his office; he had become a great deal heavier and more short of breath lately, and took a firmer hold on the stair rail.

May 1, 1844

My dearest Gitta,— It is with a certain sad, subdued feeling that I write to you this time; nay, I could even wish to characterize it by a stronger expression. It comes to my old ears as if there was a lamentation sounding over so many bright hopes bowing their heads to the ground; and I can only find consolation in the firm faith, cherished through a long life, that nothing happens save as a link in a higher wisdom.

Just as I have hitherto tried to present everything relating to Inger-Johanna as clearly before you as I could see it myself, so I find it most proper not to conceal from you the struggle which she plainly is going through against a feeling, from whose power I hope there may yet be salvation in the fortunate circumstance that it has not yet had full time to come into being and ripen in her.

It is there, and it produces pain, but more, is my hope, as a possibility, which has not put out sufficient roots, than as a reality, a living growth, which could not, without injury to her innermost being, coldly be subdued and stifled again.

But never has shrewd calculation celebrated a more sorry triumph than when the governor's wife believed that she could find a remedy by keeping the person concerned at a distance and at last even by persecuting him, in order to make it impossible for him to support himself here. When it is considered that Inger-Johanna, during all the treatment that Grip has endured for his ideas, has plainly sympathized with, almost championed them, the result should not have been difficult to foresee.

And one cold, frosty morning early this winter, Inger-Johanna came here in great mental excitement to make an examination into his condition through Jörgen. It was then also at her appeal that Jörgen asked him to teach him four hours a week.

On this occasion I saw clearly what before I had only suspected, but which had not escaped your sister-in-law's sharp eye, that Student Grip, without Inger-Johanna's having any idea of it, had engrossed her as a personality that drew her more and more.

It is of no use to conceal it; it is a crisis which must be fought through, before she finally becomes any other person's, if her position is not to be a false one, and if she is not to support a lifelong sorrow.

That the news of her betrothal has fallen like a saddening disappointment of a hope (even if a remote one) on this young man, I regard as far from improbable.

I certainly cannot forget the two serious young faces, which for a moment stood looking at each other, when they met in my room one afternoon. There was not much said.

She knew that he had been wronged and she hinted something to that effect.

"Possibly, Miss Jäger," he said harshly, while he took hold of the door-knob. "So many soap-bubbles burst."

Inger-Johanna remained standing and looking down on the floor. It was as if an entire change had come over her; I am sure it dawned upon her what he felt.

The discharge from the governor's bureau has plainly enough been welcome to many of the families which immediately after with singular quickness seized the opportunity to dismiss him as tutor. A man of such strangely discordant ideas had long been thought not quite desirable to receive. And the example had been given.

From an honest heart I offered him a loan, so that he might live in peace for two or three months and study, until he could again get places to teach;

but either he was too sore and proud, or else he thought that Inger-Johanna had a hand in it.

He has certainly taken it very much to heart that the total want of means of existence has now compelled him to give up the school, which was his pride, so that he is now in a certain way an object of ridicule, and this has capped the climax.

He goes about unoccupied, so Jörgen reports, and asks for credit at eating-houses and restaurants, where he sits out the evening and night.

I understood well enough that it was not just for the sake of her old aunt or for the thing itself, but to hear about him, that Inger-Johanna sat with me so often and learned the old-fashioned stitch with pearls and gold thread. She was in such an excited condition and so abstracted, and jumped up when Jörgen came home towards evening and, more's the pity, as often as not had been looking for him in vain to read with him.

That pale, darkly brilliant face stands so before me, Gitta, with which she one evening broke out: "Aunt—Aunt—Aunt Alette!"

It was like a hidden cry.

Where he is living now, Jörgen has not succeeded in finding out; possibly for want of means he has been turned out of his lodgings.

I narrate all this so much in detail, because it is to be believed and hoped that the severest part of the crisis, so far as she is concerned, is over now.

CHAPTER XII

Since that evening, when she felt that she had forgotten herself, she has at least not talked about him, nor, as I know certainly, addressed a word to Jörgen. She has evidently esteemed his character very highly, and has now suffered a disappointment.

It is not well to be young and have a great deal of life that can suffer. I tell you, it is as with your teeth; there is no peace until you have them all in your table drawer.

No, all this was not anything for father, Ma thought.

. . . .

Great-Ola was standing with a crowbar. There was a stone which was to be placed in the wall. But the frozen crust of earth was hard, up there on the meadow, although the sun was so roasting hot that he was obliged to wipe his forehead with his pointed cap every time he rested.

The non-commissioned officers had returned to the office during the forenoon with their pay in their pockets, one after the other; and that it was pretty bad going with holes in the highway was evident from their splashed carts, which were as if they had been dipped in the mud.

He had just got ready to put the crowbar under again, when he suddenly stopped. There was something which attracted his attention—a cariole with a post-boy walking by the side and a little yellow horse covered with mud up to its belly.

With pieces of rope for reins and wound around the cariole thills, the horse toiled up along the Gilje hills in zigzag, incessantly stopping to get breath. The sun was burning hot down there on the frozen earth.

The post down from Drevstad—he knew both the horse and the lumbering vehicle.

It was not that which would have taken his attention so seriously; but some one was sitting in it—a lady with hat and veil. He did not understand—that way of carrying the head—was n't it—

He took two or three slow, thoughtful steps, then started on the jump, and over the wall with a leap which would have touched the roof-beam in a high room.

"Why, in the Lord's name, if it is n't Inger-Johanna herself!" he ejaculated, as he suddenly stood by the side of the horse. "What will the capt—"

At the sight of her he suddenly had a misgiving that perhaps everything might not be so well.

"And such a rattle-trap!" he said, recovering himself, "is that fit for Inger-Johanna?"

"Good morning, Great-Ola, is father at home, and mother? No, I am not so very well, but shall be better now."

CHAPTER XII

She became silent again.

Great-Ola walked on, leading the horse by the reins, when Inger-Johanna drove into the yard.

There stood her father under the painting-ladder, looking up. He suddenly shaded his eyes, and was at once with her by the cariole.

"Inger-Johanna!"

She hugged him tightly out there, and the captain, dreadfully perplexed, drew her into the hall to Ma, who was standing there dumb.

"What is the matter, what is the matter, Inger-Johanna?" he burst out.

"Go in—go into the room a little, Jäger." She knew how little he could bear. "Let her talk with me first, and then we will come in to you—it is surely not anything irreparable."

"Father, Ma? Why should not father understand me?"

"Come, come, child," the captain made haste to say; he had hardly any voice left.

And she sat down there in the sitting-room with her father by her side on the sofa and her mother on a chair, and told them how she had fought and striven to make herself fancy that her life's task lay with Rönnow.

She had created for herself a whole pile of illusions.

But then, on one day — and she also knew which one — they became like extinguished lights for her

—black as coal and empty, wherever she looked—not what she had thought, not what she meant—like throwing herself into a desert.

"And aunt insisted that I should choose the pattern of my wedding dress. I think I should have gone into it blindly, with my eyes shut, nevertheless; for I thought of you, father, what you would say, and of you, mother,—and of the whole world outside, what it would say, if I thus, without any trace of reason, broke my engagement. And then I considered that everything was settled. I had thrown myself into the water and was only sinking, sinking—I had no right now to do anything else than drown. But then—"

"Well," a short ominous cough; the captain sat looking on the floor with his hands on his knees.

"Then," resumed Inger-Johanna with a low voice, still paler, and violently impressed with her subject—"Nay, there need not be any secret from you, father, and you, mother, since you otherwise would not understand me;— it came almost like a flash of lightning upon me, that for wholly one year, and perhaps for two, I had had my whole soul bound up with another."

"Who is it?"

"Grip," she whispered.

The captain had sat patiently and listened — entirely patiently — till the last word. But now he flew up and placed himself before her; he struck

CHAPTER XII

his hands together on the backs, and stretched them out, utterly without self-control.

"But, kingdom of heaven!" he broke out at last. "Where are you!—What are you thinking of? You can't for a single moment ever think of comparing such a — Grip with a man like Rönnow? —I tell you, Inger-Johanna, your father is absolutely, totally—you—you might just as well rise up and strike me dead at once."

"Listen, father!" came from Inger-Johanna; at the same moment she sprang up and stood before him. "If Thinka and the others have not saved themselves, no one shall trample on me."

Ma continued sitting with sharp, compressed face.

"Such pure insanity!" The captain struck his fist against his forehead and walked up and down the floor disconsolately. "But now I see it;" he stopped again, nodding to himself. "You have been spoiled, dreadfully spoiled—spoiled, since you were little—And then we get it again, only because I think so much of you."

"The whole world could contradict me, father. I have only my right way to go—to do as I have done—write to Rönnow, give full explanation, and tell it to aunt. And," she leaned against the sofa and looked down bitterly, as the remembrance came over her, "aunt has done what she could, I can assure you—thought, as you do, father, that it was pure insanity. She was so fond of me that she did not care how much wretchedness it was for me if the match only came off. So vain and young as I was, she thought, all she had to do was to get Grip cried down and pursued, so that he should stand without means, hemmed in on all sides without any way out, a man made an object of ridicule, who was obliged to give up his purpose—only his father over again. It was so easily done, as he fought for his opinions unsupported, and it would be taken up so readily, as she knew." She stood there so self-assured, tremblingly lost in her own thoughts, with downcast eyes and dark brows. She had become thin and slim. "And now I have come home here with more sorrow than I can tell you or explain— so full of fear——"

There was a silence during which strange emotions were working in the captain. "Do you say that we are not fond of you—will do you harm? Well, then, perhaps, I might not consider it so right hereafter, what you have done. I say perhaps; but now I tell you that, if you must do it, then we shall stand by it, just as you yourself wish in the affair. You understand it, at all events. Why, you have not even sat down, child. Let her have something to eat, Ma, at once."

He started up. There was a good deal to be got out of the way in her room, so she should not see that repairs were going on.

Chapter XIII

THE captain's house, freshly painted red, stood there on the hillside through the summer, and looked out over the country; it had become an ornament to the district.

But Great-Ola did not see how it was. Since the painting the captain was not like himself, some way or other. It did not have the right good luck with it. He came out there one time after another, and forgot what he came after, so that he must turn back again. Not a bad word to be heard from his mouth any longer, far from that, and he did not box one's ears.

The captain did not feel safe from dizziness this year. He went about continually making stops, and the one who must always go with him on his different trips over the grounds, stop when he stopped and go when he went, was Inger-Johanna. It was as if he seemed to find strength for himself in her erect carriage, and besides wanted to make sure that she was not going about grieving.

"Do you believe that she will ride or drive?" he asked Ma out in the pantry. "She stands there planting here and there and taking up and putting down in the garden; she is not accustomed to that now, Ma, you see. It seems to me, she is so serious. But can you imagine what will become of her? Huh," he sighed. "Nay, can you imagine it?" He took a ladle of whey out of the tub—"Drink plenty of whey, that thins the blood and prolongs life, Rist says—so that she can be the captain's daughter the longer here at Gilje—I have been thinking, Ma, that I am not going down to the sheriff's birthday on Thursday. Thinka is soon coming up, and— Oh, it is good to drink when one is thirsty."

On that same above named Thursday, the captain went about more than commonly silent and taciturn. Not a syllable at the dinner table, from the time he sat down till he rose again and peevishly, heavily, trudged up the stairs in order to take his after-dinner nap as it now should be, sitting and only for a moment.

He did not know whether he had closed his eyes or not; it did n't matter, either.

He rushed out of the office door—"Suppose they are now talking among themselves, Scharfenberg and the others. Just as amusing as to run the gauntlet through the whole country to travel down there." He stood absorbed before the great clothes-press out in the hall, when Inger-Johanna came up. "Will you see something?" said he—"your long boots when you were small."

She did not like to go into the housekeeping, but developed a great activity in outside affairs. For the present, the garden must be enlarged, the beds must be measured and spaded, and the hedge planted for Thinka's coming visit.

CHAPTER XIII

With a straw hat on, she was in the garden from early morning. There was such peace in being able to work in the fresh air and escaping from sitting over the sewing and thinking.

The captain went about shrinking from the drill.

Ma had several times proposed to send for Rist; but now she and Inger-Johanna in consultation determined really to do so.

Such a calming down always followed the doctor's visits.

Of course he should go to the drill-ground. A little lively marching in rank and file took off the fat so effectually and made the blood circulate as it should. "You have never yet talked about your head swimming when you were in camp, Jäger. It is just the right treatment, if you want to be allowed a glass of punch again on this side of Christmas."

While Gülcke was on the circuits, Thinka came up on a visit.

The sisters were at home again together, talking as in the old time; but neither of them wondered any longer what there might be in the outside world.

They knew that so well, both of them.

He felt so comfortable, the captain said, when he saw Thinka sitting there with her knitting-work and a novel, either out on the stairs or in the sitting-room.

"She is satisfied with her lot now, is n't she?" he said to Ma.

He came back to it so often; it was as if he had a secret disquietude on that point. By getting an insight into the matter through Inger-Johanna, he had to a degree got his eyes opened, at least to the extent of a suspicion, as to the possibility that a woman could be unhappy in a good match.

Then, on the other hand, his constant consolation was that such as Inger-Johanna must be exceptional examples of humanity — with her commanding nature and intolerance of living under any one's thumb.

But ordinary girls were not endowed with such lofty feelings and thoughts — and Thinka was, as it were, made for giving way and submitting to some one.

All the same, the question still lay and writhed like a worm in his stomach.

"Inger-Johanna!" said Thinka out on the stairs, "notice father, how unnerved he looks now, he is walking down there by the garden fence — and he is all the time forgetting his pipe; it is not half smoked up before it goes out."

"So you think he is changed," said Inger-Johanna, musing and resuming the conversation, up in their room in the evening. "Poor father; it is so absolutely impossible for him to get over it; I was destined to be a parade horse. But do you believe he would now demand it again of any of us?"

"You are strong, Inger-Johanna, and I suppose you are right. But he has become so good," Thinka said, sighing; "and it is that which makes me uneasy."

As the time drew nearer, he went about, dreading more and more to go to the camp, so that Ma finally began to believe that perhaps it was not advisable for him to go, since he had himself so little courage or desire for it. During the day, he would walk about quite alone, so that he might come to shun people altogether.

And the first real gleam of light she had seen for a long time on his countenance was when she, notwithstanding, proposed that he write to the army surgeon for a certificate of sickness.

It went on smoothly enough after it was first set in motion. And yet he seemed to repent it, so to speak, when his leave of absence actually lay upon his desk.

He went about annoyed and thought about them all down there. Now Captain Vonderthan would naturally spoil the men on the drill-ground; and this one and that one was speculating, he supposed, even now, on whether he would not possibly go upon half pay. But he would disappoint them by lasting as long as possible, if he should drink whey the year round.

The time, which was so absorbing and disturbing to his mind, when the drill was taking place, was over at last, and he had already, through Ma's persuasion, by degrees reconciled himself to a possible trip to the principal parish, when a scrap of a letter from Jörgen was brought in the mail, which put them all in great distress.

He could not endure any longer to sit there as the poorest in his class, and had shipped on board a vessel which was going to sail that evening for England. From there he hoped to find some means of getting over to America, where he would try to become a blacksmith or a wheelwright or something else. He would not fail to write home to his dear parents what his fate was.

"There, Ma," said the captain with a deep, trembling voice, when at last he had got over his stupefaction a little, "that Grip has been expensive for us. It is nothing but his teaching."

. . . .

The autumn was already far advanced. The snow had come and gone twice, and had now been swept off by the wind from the slippery, hard frozen road. The slopes and mountains were white, with red and yellow tones of the frost-touched leaves of the leafy forest still showing in many places, and the lake down below was shining coldly blue, ready to freeze over.

CHAPTER XIII

There was a thundering over the country road hard with frost, so it waked the echoes in the quiet October day; one crow was standing, and another started up from the hedge-post at the sound.

It was the wheels of a cariole, and in it was sitting, with a long whip hanging down behind his back, in cloak and large overshoes, the Captain of Gilje.

He had been ten miles down and had his yearly settlement with Bardon Kleven.

It is true, the bailiff had not been willing to let him go out of the house without compelling him to taste a little brandy in a small tumbler, with a little ale in addition, and a little something to eat. But he had been prudent. It was almost the only trip he had made away from home for a long time, except his visit to the sheriff.

Old Svarten ran over the long, flat stretches in the heavy, strong trot to which he was accustomed; the road showed that he was sharp shod with full caulks. He knew that he was not to stop till he had done the three miles to the foot of the steep ascent up the Gilje hills.

It was probably because he was newly shod, and the lumps of mud were so large and were frozen hard; but now he stumbled.

It was the first time it had happened. Perhaps he felt it himself, for he kept on at a brisker trot — but then slackened up by degrees. He felt that the reins were loose and slack; their folds fell longer and longer down over his shoulders.

The whip-lash hung down as before over the captain's back, only still more slantingly.

He had begun to feel such cold shivers, just as if he had suddenly got cold all over—and now he had become so sleepy—had such a longing for a nap.

He saw the reins, the ears, and the hanging mane over the neck of Svarten nodding up and down before him, and the ground beneath him flying away—

It was just as if a crow flew up and made it dark right over his face; but he could not get his arm up to catch it—so let it be.

And there stood the grain-poles, like crooked old witches, crouched down—they wanted to avenge themselves—with straw forelocks they resisted him more and more like goblins and would forbid him to get his arms up to take the reins and drive to Gilje. They were swarming between heaven and earth, as it were, swimming, dancing—were bright and dark. Then there was something like a shout or a crash from somewhere. There was Inger-Johanna coming—

Svarten had got the reins quite down over his forelegs; a little more and he would be stepping on them.

From the gentle trot, into which he had at last fallen, he began to walk.

CHAPTER XIII

Then he turned his head round — and remained standing in the middle of the road.

The whip-lash hung down as before. The captain sat there immovable with his head a little tipped back —

They were still on the level, and Svarten stood patiently looking toward the Gilje hill, which lay a bit farther on, until he turned his head round again two or three times and looked into the cariole.

Now he began to paw on the ground with one forefoot, harder and harder — so that the lumps flew about.

Then he neighed.

A good hour later, in the twilight, there was a conversation in an undertone out in the yard, and the sound of cariole wheels which moved slowly.

Great-Ola was called down to the gate by the man down yonder at the Sörgaard; he had met the cariole with the captain down in the road.

"What is it?" Ma's voice was heard to say through the darkness from the porch.

. . . .

At the entrance of the churchyard, a week later, old Svarten and young Svarten stood before an empty sleigh.

A salute before and after the lowering into the ground informed the parish that here lay Captain Peter Wennechen Jäger.

Chapter XIV

ABOUT twenty years had passed, and the traffic down in the country store and inn showed an entirely different style both in building and goods. There had also begun to be a route for travellers and tourists in the summer up through the valley.

The snow drifted, so that it lay high up on the steps this Sunday afternoon.

But in the little warm room behind the shop there was jollity. He had come up again, he, the delightful Grip; and now he was sitting there with the shopkeeper, the bailiff's man, and the execution-server.

Only let him get a little something to drink.

"Your health, you old execution-horse!" came in Grip's voice — "When I think of all those whom you have taken the skin off without ever getting any part in the roast, I can get up a kind of sympathy for you; we are both of us cheated souls."

"Although I have not acquired the learning and sciences"—began the gray-headed man who had been spoken to, somewhat irritated—"I insist on—"

"Everything lawful, yes — oh — oh — never mind that, Reierstad. Consider that science is the sea of infinity, and a few drops more or less do not count either for or against. Just peep out a little into the starry night, and you will have a suspicion

CHAPTER XIV

that the whole of the planet, my friend, on which you parade in such a very small crevice, is only one pea in the soup—soup, I say—it is all the same. Is n't that so, Mr.—Mr. Simensen?"

He always appealed to the shop boy, who, with his small pig's eyes, smiled very superciliously and was evidently flattered.

"And in regard to the last information, one ought to have a little something to reinforce the oil in the lamp with, Sir."

It was the execution-server who had stood treat first—a pint and a half bottle of spirits.

The execution-server had a kind of ancient deferential respect for Grip. He knew that he had belonged to the higher sphere, and that he still, whenever he liked, might show himself in the houses both of the sheriff and of old Rist, places which he never left without improvements in his outfit.

"I will confide a secret to you, Reierstad. If you are a little of a genius, then you must drink—at least it was true in my time. There was great havoc on that kind, you see, on account of the vacuum. Did you not notice something of that?"

"Hi, hi, hi," neighed Simensen.

"Yes, you understand what I mean, Simensen? —A good glass of punch extract in this frost—of yours in the shop—would taste so good now, would n't it? I am not at present flush of money; but if you will have the goodness to put it down."

Simensen caught the idea, of course. "All right, then."

"As you grease the wheels, the carriage goes, you know very well, my dear Simensen—and, well,—there comes the fluid.—Do you want to know why we drink?"

"Oh, it can't be so very difficult to fathom that."

"No, no; but yet it may perhaps be placed in a higher light, which a man like you will not fail to appreciate—you know there is a great objection to new illumination fluids, besides—you see, hm!" He seated himself comfortably—"You live in a thin coat and cold, poor conditions—are ashamed of yourself at heart—feel that you are sinking as a man, day by day. If there is a discussion, you don't dare to assert yourself; if you are placed at a table, you don't dare to speak. And then—only two drams—two glasses of poor brandy for spectacles to see through—and *ein, zwei, drei, marsch!* The whole world is another!—You become yourself, feel that you are in that health and vigor which you were once intended for; your person becomes independent, proud, and bold; the words fall from your lips; your ideas are bright; people admire. The two glasses—only two glasses—I do not refuse, however, the three, four, five, and six, your health! —make the difference—you know what the difference is, Simensen!—between his healthy and his sick man, while the man whom the world struck

CHAPTER XIV

down—well, yes—But the two glasses carry him always farther—farther—inexorably farther, you see—until he ends in the workhouse. That was a big syllogism."

"Yes, it certainly was," said Simensen, nodding to the execution-server; "it took half a bottle with it."

Grip sat there mumbling.

The strong drink had plainly got more and more hold on him; he had been out in the cold the whole day. His boots were wet and in bad condition. But he continued to drink; almost alone he had disposed of the punch extract.

"Come, come, don't sit there so melancholy—or there won't be any more to get," Simensen prodded him.

"No, no—no, no—more syllogisms, you mean—something Reierstad also can understand." He nodded his head in quiet, dull self-communion. "Came across an emaciated, pale child, who was crying so utterly helplessly down here. There is much that screams helplessly—you know, Reierstad!—if one has once got an ear for the music, and has not a river of tears—there, you drink, drink. Give me the bottle."

"It were best to get him to bed over in the servants' room, now," suggested Simensen.

"Perhaps the pig is drunk," muttered Grip.

Monday morning he was off again, before daylight, without having tasted anything; he was shy so early, before he had got his first dram to stiffen him up.

Grip had his own tactics. He was known over very nearly the whole of the country south of the Dovrefjeld.

As he had had fits of drinking and going on a spree, so he had had corresponding periods when he had lived soberly in the capital, studying and giving instruction. Again and again he awoke the most well-grounded hopes in his few old comrades and friends who remained there. A man with such a talent for teaching and such a remarkable gift for grasping the roots of words and the laws of language, not only in Greek and Latin, but right up into the Sanscrit, might possibly even yet attain to something. Based on his total abstinence for three and four months and his own strong self-control, they would already begin to speak of bringing about his installation at some school of a higher grade, when all at once, unexpectedly, it was again reported that he had disappeared from the city.

Then he would pop up again after the lapse of some weeks—entirely destitute, in one of the country districts, shaking and thin and worn from drink, from exposure, from lying in outhouses and in haylofts, seldom undressed and in a proper bed.

Along in the afternoon he appeared at the sheriff's house.

CHAPTER XIV

Gülcke was the only one of the functionaries of his time who still kept his office, after Rist had left. He was still there, nursed by a careful wife, who had ever surrounded him with a padding of pillows, visible and invisible.

Grip knew what he was doing; he wanted to find the mistress, while the sheriff was in his office.

She was sitting in an easy chair snugly behind the double windows in the sitting-room with her knitting-work and *The Wandering Jew* before her, while her clever sister Thea, an unmarried woman now in the thirties, was looking after the dinner out in the kitchen.

Thinka took the care of the house upon herself after Miss Gülcke's death, and was her old husband's support and crutch unweariedly the whole twenty-four hours together.

And these greasy, worn books of fiction from the city, with numbers on their backs, were the little green spot left for her to pass her own life on.

Like so many other women of those times, to whom reality had not left any other escape than to take any man who could support her, she lived in these novels—in the midst of the most harshly creaking commonplaces—a highly strained life of fancy. There she imagined the passions she herself might have had. There were loves and hates, there were two noble hearts—in spite of everything—happily united; or she consoled picturesque heroes, who in despair were gazing into the billows.

There — in the clouds — was continued the life with its unquenchable thirst of the heart and of the spirit for which reality had not given any firm foothold — and there the matronly figure which had become somewhat large, cozily round and plump, and which was once the small, slender Thinka, transferred her still unforgotten Aas from one heroic form to another — from Emilie Carlén to James, from Walter Scott to Bulwer, from Alexander Dumas to Eugène Sue.

There in her domestic, bustling sister's place lay the sewing, with a ray of sunshine on the chair.

The dark inlaid sewing-table was Thea's inheritance from Ma. And the silver thimble, with the shell old and worn thin inside and out, broken and cracked at the top and on the edges, she used and saved, because her mother had used it all her time. It stood, left behind like a monument to Ma — to all the weary stitches — and pricks — of her honorably toiling, self-sacrificing — shall we call it life?

It was more at a pressure than by regularly knocking that the door to the sitting-room was opened, and Grip cautiously entered.

"You, Grip? No, no, not by the door, sit down up there by the window. Then my sister will get you a little something to eat, — oh, you can manage to eat a little bread and butter and salt meat, can't you? Well, so you are up this way, Grip?"

CHAPTER XIV

"Seeking a chance to teach, I may say, Mrs. Gülcke," was the evasive reply. "I am told you have heard from Jörgen over in America," he hastily added, to get away from the delicate subject.

"Yes, just think: Jörgen is a well-to-do, rich manager of a machine-shop over in Savannah. He has now written two letters and wants to have his eldest sister come over; but Inger-Johanna is not seeking for happiness any more —" she added with a peculiar emphasis.

There was a silence.

Grip, with a very trembling hand, placed the plate of bread and butter, which the maid had brought, on the sewing-table. He had drunk the dram on the side of the plate. There was a twitching about his lips.

"It gives me pleasure, exceeding great pleasure," he uttered in a voice which he controlled with difficulty. "You see, Mrs. Gülcke, that Jörgen has amounted to something I count as one of the few rare blades of grass that have grown up out of my poor life."

Sleigh-bells sounded out in the road; a sleigh glided into the yard.

"The judge's," Thinka said.

Grip comprehended that he would not be wanted just now, and rose.

Thinka hastened out into a side room and came in again with a dollar bill — "Take it, Grip — a little assistance till you get some pupils."

His hand hesitated a little before he took it. "One,—must—must—" He seized his cap and went out.

Down by the gate he stopped a little, and looked back. The window had been thrown open there.

"Airing out after Grip," he muttered bitterly, while he took the direction of the valley, with his comforter high up around his neck and his cap, which down in the main parish had replaced his old, curled up felt hat, down over his ears; in the cold east wind he protected his hands in the pockets of his old thin coat, which was flapping about his emaciated form.

It was not an uncommon route, whither he went over the mountains in his widely extended rambles in the summer, or, as now, in the short, dark midwinter, when he was obliged to confine himself to the highway.

This country district had an attraction for him, as it were; he listened and watched everywhere he came for even the least bit of what he could catch up about Inger-Johanna, while he carefully avoided her vicinity.

"The young lady of Gilje," as she was called, lived in a little house up there, which she had bought with one of the four thousand dollars that old Aunt Alette had given to her by will.

She kept a school for the children of the region,

CHAPTER XIV

and read with those of the captain, the newly settled doctor, and the bailiff.

And now she had many boys to care for, whom she had got places in the country round about, while in the course of years she had striven to put several young geniuses from the neighborhood in the way of getting on down in the cities.

She was imperious, and gave occasion for people's talk by her unusually independent conduct; but to her face she met pure respect. She was still, at her fortieth year, delicate and slender, with undiminished, even if more quiet, fire in her eyes, and hair black as a raven.

She sought for talents in the children like four-leaved clover on the hills, as she was said to have expressed it; and when Grip, down at Thinka's, talked of Jörgen's happy escape from his surroundings as one of the few green leaves in his life, he then suppressed the most secret thought he cherished, that her little school was an offshoot propagated by his ideas.

In the twilight the next afternoon a form stole up to the fence around her schoolroom—the longing to catch, if possible, a glimpse of her drove him nearer and nearer.

Now he was standing close to the window.

An obscure form now and then moved before it.

An uncertain gleam was playing about in there from the mouth of the stove. The lamp was not yet lighted, and he heard the voice of a boy reciting something which he had learned by heart, but did not know well; it sounded like verse—it must be the children from the captain's house.

The entry door was open, and a little later he was standing in it, listening breathlessly.

He heard her voice—her voice.

"Recite it, Ingeborg—boys are so stupid in such things."

It was a poem from the Norwegian history. Ingeborg's voice came clearly:

And that was young Queen Gyda,
The flower in King Harald's spring—
Walks yet so proud a maiden
Over the mountain ling?

Highborn was she and haughty,
Her seat she would not share;
The Hordaland damsels away she sent,
And the Rogaland girls must fare.

She willed a kingdom united
To the outermost skerrie bare,
A king for a queen, the whole of a man
For a maid—and none to share.

He stood as if rooted to the floor, until he heard Inger-Johanna say, "I will now light the lamp, and give you your lessons for to-morrow."

CHAPTER XIV

Immediately he was away before the window.

He saw her head in the glow of the lamp just lighted—that purity in the shape of her eyebrows and in the lines of her face—that unspeakably beautiful, serious countenance, only even more characteristically stamped—that old erect bearing with the tall, firm neck.

It was a picture which had stood within him all these years—of her who should have been his if he had attained to what he ought to have attained in life—if it had offered him what it should have—and if he himself had been what he ought to have been.

He stood there stupefied as if in a dizzy intoxication—and then went away with long strides, when he heard the children coming out into the entry.

His feet bore him without his knowing it.

Now he was far down the Gilje hills, and the moonlight began to shine over the ridges. He still hurried on; his blood was excited; he saw—almost talked with her.

A sleigh came trotting slowly behind him with the bells muffled by the frost.

It was old Rist, who was sitting nodding in his fur coat, exhausted by what he had enjoyed at Gilje.

"If you are going over the lake, Grip, jump on behind," he said by way of salutation, after looking at him a little.

"I tell you, if you could only leave off drinking," he began to admonish—

Before the lamp thus—it ran in Grip's thoughts —she set the milky shade slowly down over the chimney, and a gleam passed over her delicate mouth and chin— the dark, closely fitting dress— and the forehead, while she bowed her magnificent head—she looked up—straight towards the window—

"And if you will only try to resist it—at the time the fit comes on—which is the same as the very Satan himself."

Grip was not inclined to hear any more, and it was cold to hang on over the lake.

He jumped off and let old Rist continue his talk in the idea that he was standing behind him.

It was a cold, biting wind out on the ice.

For a while he saw his own shadow, with his hands in his coat pockets, moving away, while the moon sailed through the clouds— the lamp shone so warmly on her face—

. . . .

Three days afterwards, towards evening, Inger-Johanna stood at the window looking out. Her breast heaved with strong emotion.

Grip had died of pneumonia down at the Lövviggaard.

She had been down and taken care of him till

now she had come home—talked with him, heard herself live in his wild raving, and had received his last intelligent look before it was quenched. . . .

The moon was so cold and clear in the heavens. The whole landscape with the mountains and all the great pure forms shone magically white in the frost—white as in the snow-fields of the lofty mountains. . . .

"The power of the spirit is great," she said, sighing in sorrowful, yet trembling meditation—"he gave me something to live on."

THE END

PUBLICATIONS OF
THE AMERICAN-SCANDINAVIAN FOUNDATION

COMMITTEE ON PUBLICATIONS

WILLIAM HENRY SCHOFIELD, Professor of Comparative Literature in Harvard University, *Chairman*

WILLIAM WITHERLE LAWRENCE, Professor of English in Columbia University

CHARLES S. PETERSON, Publisher, Chicago

HENRY GODDARD LEACH, Secretary of the Foundation

SCANDINAVIAN CLASSICS

I. *Comedies by Holberg: Jeppe of the Hill, The Political Tinker, Erasmus Montanus*
Translated by OSCAR JAMES CAMPBELL, JR., and FREDERIC SCHENCK

II. *Poems by Tegnér: The Children of the Lord's Supper and Frithiof's Saga*
Translated by HENRY WADSWORTH LONGFELLOW and W. LEWERY BLACKLEY

III. *Poems and Songs by Björnstjerne Björnson*
Translated in the original metres, with an Introduction and Notes, by ARTHUR HUBBELL PALMER

IV. *Master Olof by August Strindberg*
An historical play, translated, with an Introduction, by EDWIN BJÖRKMAN

V. *The Prose Edda by Snorri Sturluson*
Translated from old Icelandic, with an Introduction and Notes, by ARTHUR GILCHRIST BRODEUR

VI. *Modern Icelandic Plays by Jóhann Sigurjónsson: Eyvind of the Hills and The Hraun Farm*
Translated by Henninge Krohn Schanche

VII. *Marie Grubbe: A Lady of the Seventeenth Century by J. P. Jacobsen*
An historical romance, translated, with an Introduction, by Hanna Astrup Larsen

VIII. *Arnljot Gelline by Björnstjerne Björnson*
A Norse epic, translated by William Morton Payne

IX. *Anthology of Swedish Lyrics, from 1750 to 1915*
Selections from the greatest of Swedish lyrists, translated by Charles Wharton Stork

X & XI. *Gösta Berling's Saga by Selma Lagerlöf*
The English translation of Lillie Tudeer, completed and carefully edited

XII. *Sara Videbeck (Det går an), and The Chapel, by C. J. L. Almquist*
A Sentimental Journey with a practical ending, and the Tale of a Curate, translated, with an Introduction, by Adolph Burnett Benson

XIII. *Niels Lyhne by J. P. Jacobsen*
A psychological novel, translated by Hanna Astrup Larsen

XIV. *The Family at Gilje: A Domestic Story of the Forties, by Jonas Lie*
Translated by Samuel Coffin Eastman, with an Introduction by Julius Emil Olson

XV & XVI. *The Charles Men by Verner von Heidenstam*
Tales from the exploits of Charles XII, translated by CHARLES WHARTON STORK, with an Introduction by FREDRIK BÖÖK

Price $2.00 each

THE SCANDINAVIAN MONOGRAPHS

I. *The Voyages of the Norsemen to America*
A complete exposition, with illustrations and maps, by WILLIAM HOVGAARD

Price $4.00

II. *Ballad Criticism in Scandinavia and Great Britain during the Eighteenth Century*
A comparative study, by SIGURD BERNARD HUSTVEDT

Price $3.00

III. *The King's Mirror*
A famous treatise, translated from the Norwegian of the Thirteenth Century, with an Historical Introduction, by LAURENCE MARCELLUS LARSON

Price $3.00

IV. *The Heroic Legends of Denmark*
Revised and expanded for this edition by the author, the late AXEL OLRIK, in collaboration with the translator, LEE M. HOLLANDER

Price $5.00

In Preparation

V. *A History of Scandinavian Art*
By CARL G. LAURIN of Sweden, EMIL HANNOVER of Denmark, and JENS THIIS of Norway; with a foreword by CHRISTIAN BRINTON

THE AMERICAN–SCANDINAVIAN REVIEW

An Illustrated Magazine, presenting the progress of life and literature in Sweden, Denmark, and Norway

Price $2.00 a year

For information regarding the above publications, address the

SECRETARY OF THE AMERICAN-SCANDINAVIAN FOUNDATION

25 West 45th Street, New York City

LaVergne, TN USA
16 March 2011
220421LV00005B/81/P